Peer Review of Teaching

Peer Review of Teaching
A Sourcebook

SECOND EDITION

Nancy Van Note Chism

Indiana University–Purdue University Indianapolis

With Contributions by
Grady W. Chism, III

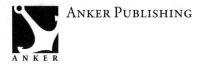 ANKER PUBLISHING

ANKER

Published by Jossey-Bass
A Wiley Imprint
989 Market Street, San Francisco, CA 94103-1741   www.josseybass.com

Jossey-Bass books and products are available through most bookstores. To contact Jossey-Bass directly call our Customer Care Department within the U.S. at 800-956-7739, outside the U.S. at 317-572-3986, or fax 317-572-4002.

Jossey-Bass also publishes its books in a variety of electronic formats. Some content that appears in print may not be available in electronic books.

Composition by Julie Phinney
Cover design by Dutton & Sherman Design

Library of Congress Cataloging-in-Publication Data

Chism, Nancy Van Note.
     Peer review of teaching: a sourcebook/Nancy Van Note Chism; with contributions by
Grady W. Chism, III. — 2nd ed.
          p. cm.
Includes bibliographical references and index.
ISBN 978-1-933371-21-4
     1. College teachers—Ratings of. 2. Peer review. I. Chism, Grady W. II. Title.

LB2333.C49 2007
378.1'22—dc22   2007009092

Printed in the United States of America
FIRST EDITION
PB Printing   10 9 8 7 6 5 4 3 2 1

Dedicated to

Francis William Van Note
Lillian McSpiritt Van Note

Parents extraordinaire

Table of Contents

About the Author

Nancy Van Note Chism is professor of higher education in the Indiana University School of Education at Indiana University–Purdue University Indianapolis (IUPUI), where she teaches courses in qualitative research, professional development, and college teaching and learning. Between 1999 and 2006, she was associate vice chancellor for academic affairs and associate dean of the faculties at IUPUI, providing leadership for faculty hiring and advancement functions such as promotion and tenure, awards, and faculty development. Her work in organizational development included administrative development and physical spaces for learning.

Previously, Dr. Chism was director of faculty and TA development at The Ohio State University and an adjunct faculty member in the university's College of Education. She has directed or participated in several major funded projects, sponsored by the Pew Charitable Trusts, Lumina Foundation, National Science Foundation, Lilly Foundation, and Fund for the Improvement of Postsecondary Education. She is past president of the Professional and Organizational Development Network in Higher Education and is a recipient of the Bob Pierleoni Spirit of POD Award.

Dr. Chism is the author of 60 edited books, book chapters, and journal articles on teaching and learning in higher education and developing faculty and teaching assistants as teachers, with particular emphasis on multicultural teaching, instructional technology, learning environments, and program evaluation. She has consulted on more than 50 campuses in the United States and abroad. Dr. Chism received a B.A. in English from Fordham University, an M.A.T. in English and education from Smith College, and a Ph.D. in educational policy and leadership from The Ohio State University.

Foreword

I am honored to have been invited to write the foreword for this second edition of Nancy Chism's fine book, *Peer Review of Teaching*. I do so with mixed feelings, however, for the foreword of the first edition was written by my good friend, Bob Menges, who died shortly after writing it. I am inadequate to fill Bob's shoes, but I enjoyed reading *Peer Review of Teaching* and am happy to pay tribute to its value.

Peer review of teaching is usually carried out in an evaluative context, sometimes from formative evaluation intended to help the reviewed faculty member to improve, but more often as a source of evidence for promotion or salary decisions. Any evaluation that can have possible negative consequences is threatening and likely to be resisted. It is not surprising that student ratings of teaching, also commonly used by administrators or personnel committees as evidence of teaching effectiveness, have generated more than 2,000 articles pro and con.

Peer review of teaching has not been studied so extensively, but there is a research literature, and most administrators and personnel committees are not familiar with the findings. Nancy Chism's book not only summarizes that research but also provides helpful guidelines to committees on establishing appropriate goals for peer review. In addition, she gives useful advice about how to carry out peer review of teaching.

Professor Chism is uniquely well qualified to write about peer review of teaching since she has not only been a teacher but also an administrator and an expert in faculty development. In addition, she has lectured or conducted workshops at many colleges and universities and has had an opportunity to observe both good and bad systems of peer evaluation.

In his foreword to the first edition, Bob Menges suggested some expectations of teachers under review:

- Teachers choose materials that best convey their teaching strengths and their efforts at improvement.
- Teachers reflect on their teaching activities and justify them to reviewers, thus revealing their assumptions and their knowledge of relevant theory and research.

- Teachers defend the consistency between major elements of a course. Are course activities consistent with stated goals? Do procedures for evaluation match course activities and reflect course goals?
- Teachers try to reconcile discrepancies among sources of evidence, including information from the teacher, comments from peers, and evaluations from students.
- Teachers consider whether their approaches and materials deserve dissemination to others. (pp. ix–x)

He also had suggestions for reviewers:

- Colleagues decide what aspects of teaching can best be reviewed by peers.
- Colleagues decide how much time and effort are to be devoted to reviewing their colleagues.
- Colleagues seek consensus about the level of achievement that is required for teaching to be judged successful.
- Colleagues confront their own assumptions and practices about teaching and learning, possibly making changes in light of their experiences as reviewers. (p. x)

Good, timeless advice!

W. J. McKeachie
Professor Emeritus, Department of Psychology
University of Michigan

Preface to the Second Edition

Over the course of the past decade or so, some important thinking about faculty teaching and its appraisal has begun to influence action. The work of Ernest Boyer, Gene Rice, Pat Hutchings, Lee Shulman, Mary Huber, Dan Bernstein, and others has helped us to think about teaching as a scholarly act, and an interesting one at that. These scholars have also emphasized the connection between teaching and learning, shifting the focus of attention from the personal act of the teacher to the less threatening and ultimately more important subject of student outcomes.

Along with this shift in thinking have come recommendations for practice. Ideas for making teaching the subject of common and open discussion within the department setting, for promoting reflection and inquiry through such vehicles as course portfolios, and for developing reasonable and comprehensive ways of assessing teaching are being shared and implemented. Alongside the developmental approaches to peer review, the bottom-line need to make personnel decisions still exists, and this volume tries to accommodate both.

Although these general improvements in the context for peer review have occurred, reservations about its use persist. Since the publication in 1999 of the first edition of *Peer Review of Teaching: A Sourcebook,* I have had the opportunity to visit many campuses in the United States and abroad. My sense is that although administrators at most colleges and universities demonstrate a periodic interest in peer review of teaching, few institutions have developed comprehensive and enduring programs. Strong reservations about peer review—and faculty evaluation in general—continue, and not without reason, since peer review of teaching can be handled very poorly and lead to unwarranted judgments. This new edition is issued in the spirit of addressing those shortcomings and enabling improved practice.

Changes in this edition include a general updating and incorporation of new ideas and references from the literature as well as new sections throughout. It is interesting to note that most of the newer sources are overviews in books or chapters of books, rather than empirical studies in journals, indicating that peer review has not been a popular topic of research. Nevertheless, some good new work has been done in conceptualizing peer review and the development of faculty evaluation systems. Notations on the specific ways in which new ideas have been incorporated are contained in the introduction on the volume's organization that follows.

Organization

Part I: An Overview of Peer Review situates peer review within the general context of the evaluation of teaching and considers ways of developing and implementing a system of peer review. Chapter 1 defines peer review, grounds it in evaluation theory, and addresses the arguments for and reservations against peer review. New to this edition is material on the several contexts in which peer review is used in the evaluation of teaching. Chapters 2 and 3 discuss setting up a system of peer review. A new tool to assess readiness is included, as well as a discussion of common pitfalls of peer review systems. Chapter 2 includes a new extended example of the approach used by the University of Saskatchewan. Chapter 3 includes more emphasis on criteria for assessing teaching, as well as tables to prompt discussion of criteria, evidence, and standards—the heart of a peer review system. Chapter 4 details the goals of peer review of teaching systems and the roles that various actors play in the process. A new table illustrating examples of feedback is included.

Part II: Resources and Forms presents information on the various approaches used in peer review of teaching and includes sample forms that can be used as models or to stimulate discussion during the development of a system. Chapters 5 and 6 focus on peer review of course materials and observation of classroom teaching.

The most notable change in this edition is a new chapter on peer review within special contexts for teaching, Chapter 7. It is easy to fall into the pattern of assuming that peer review occurs within traditional settings in which the instructor uses common approaches. Much teaching, however, is done in clinics, studios, and practice settings. The turn to active engagement in learning has also led to increased use of problem-based learning, the case study method, and other approaches that traditional forms for peer review do not address. Similarly, the explosion of the use of instructional technology calls for an articulation of new approaches to evaluating web-based instruction, which are outlined in this chapter.

Chapter 8 updates the first edition's discussion of peer review of teaching leadership efforts and the scholarship of teaching and learning. It includes a new example of a form that may be used. Chapter 9 expands considerably on the previous treatment of portfolios, including more information on course portfolios and two additional forms from the literature that might be used to review portfolios.

Chapter 10 presents guiding principles, a review of the main points of the book, and an updated source list.

Like the first book, this edition of *Peer Review of Teaching: A Sourcebook* is offered in the hope that providing examples and suggestions will not reduce the important work of peer review to mere forms or rigid procedures, but will empower faculty to articulate criteria and standards, perform the reviews systematically and thoughtfully, and realize that engaging in peer review is an approachable and worthwhile professional task. It aspires to build on the work of those who have so eloquently described teaching as scholarly work and echoes their call for communities of practice on teaching.

My interest in peer review of teaching was prompted by hearing continual complaints about student ratings of instruction during my years in faculty development. Although I have always believed that students are a necessary part of assessing teaching, an essential part of my response to these complaints has been to push for a better balance among the sources of judgment and types of approaches to collecting and examining information on teaching performance through advocating for peer review. It strikes me that as a developer, I can help with describing *how* peer review might be approached, thereby facilitating access for those who had not previously engaged in this work. I hope that this volume does illuminate peer review for many and that the ideas it prompts blossom into thoughtful and communal examination of the scholarly act that is so central to our work—teaching.

Acknowledgments

I am indebted in the development of this edition to my husband and best critic, Grady William Chism III, who not only contributed his usual thoughts in his self-professed role of "faculty curmudgeon" but collected and summarized the information on peer review of teaching in medical settings and provided substantive suggestions on the treatment of laboratory teaching and advising of student research. I also acknowledge the continuing influence of Christine Stanley, professor and associate dean of the College of Education at Texas A&M University, whose work with me on the first edition carries through to the present one. Finally, I am grateful to William M. Plater, former dean of the faculties at Indiana University–Purdue University Indianapolis (IUPUI), who prompted me to share in his leadership for faculty advancement at IUPUI, which brought me into occasions for thinking about peer review regularly. I also thank the leaders of many campuses who invited me to talk with them and their faculty about peer review of teaching. The learning I gained through these experiences led me to actualize many of my thoughts on the topic and to set them out for others in this new edition.

Nancy Van Note Chism
Professor of Higher Education
Indiana University School of Education
Indiana University–Purdue University Indianapolis

Part I

An Overview of Peer Review

Chapter 1

Developing a Rationale and Understanding of Peer Review

Today's colleges and universities are educating more and different learners, striving to support economic development, addressing globalization, and attending to a host of professional and societal needs. At the same time, they are facing pressures for increased accountability, access, and productivity in the face of decreased resources and support. Faculty report that their work has become more stressful, and the composition of the faculty has changed, with larger numbers of entrants assuming part-time and nontenure-track positions (Blackburn & Lawrence, 1995; Gmelch, 1993; Menges & Associates, 1999; Rice, Sorcinelli, & Austin, 2000; Robertson, 2003; Schuster & Finkelstein, 2006). In the face of disappointing retention and graduation rates and employer dissatisfaction with the performance of college graduates, faculty teaching has come under heightened scrutiny.

Teaching has also received more positive attention in the past decade, a time when the *scholarship of teaching and learning* has become a commonplace term. Thanks to the influence of the Carnegie Foundation for the Advancement of Teaching and the former American Association for Higher Education, faculty across the nation have contemplated the scholarly nature of their teaching, and many have approached their work in more informed ways and actively inquired into its practice (Huber, 2004; Huber & Hutchings, 2005; Hutchings, 2000).

All of these developments influence the ways in which colleges and universities are evaluating teaching, increasing both the urgency and richness of the discussion. Evaluation of teaching in higher education has long been the subject of scholarly attention. The literature on one subtopic alone—the use of student ratings forms in the evaluation of teaching—purportedly constitutes the most voluminous component of higher education research. But evaluation is a complex and emotion-charged activity; even though the scholarship is well developed, day-to-day practice continues to struggle.

Within this broad context of teacher evaluation, the status of peer review of teaching is troubled as well. Although colleges and universities have long operated on a tradition of collegial governance, decision-making and mentoring with respect to growth in teaching have created chronic anxieties. This chapter will define peer review of teaching, summarize the general implications of the research on the evaluation of teaching, then present the background for peer review of teaching: the rationale for peer review and the issues involved in discussions of peer review of teaching.

Definition of Peer Review of Teaching

Peer review of teaching is informed colleague judgment about faculty teaching for either fostering improvement or making personnel decisions. The elements of this definition will all be explored in this volume. First, the notion of informed judgment implies a systematic act, based on appropriate evidence and thought processes. Most of this volume will revolve around how to identify, collect, and assess this evidence. The word *colleague* suggests not only someone of similar professional status, but in this context, a person who is qualified by expertise or training to serve as a knowledgeable judge. This volume will discuss choosing appropriate colleagues and preparing them to serve as peer reviewers. Finally, the two purposes of peer review are an important part of the definition and must be considered in discussions of peer review. A review of the literature on the evaluation of teaching included in this chapter will illuminate this distinction.

Contexts of Peer Review

Although peer review of teaching is generally associated with classroom observation, it is important to state emphatically at the beginning of this volume that classroom observation is only one method of peer review of teaching, and a very limited one at that. Peer review of teaching is involved in many routine activities at colleges and universities:

- Hiring faculty
- Establishing communities of practice
- Coaching faculty
- Reviewing faculty for salary increases

- Deciding on contract renewals
- Determining faculty assignments
- Judging promotion and tenure cases
- Approving teaching sabbatical requests
- Choosing teaching award winners
- Conducting post-tenure reviews

Examples of these uses will be included later in this chapter after some basic distinctions are provided.

The nature of faculty oversight of the profession of college teaching requires the involvement of peers in advocating, mentoring, and decision-making activities related to this central faculty role. Peer review is imbued in current approaches to faculty work. It is extremely important, then, that the quality of peer review of teaching be examined and supported. To do less jeopardizes the effectiveness of all of the activities listed above.

Any discussion of peer review of teaching must also note the different environments in which the review takes place as well as differences in the appointment types of those who are doing the teaching. For example, review of teaching of technical material, as opposed to conceptual subject matter or performance skills, must take into account the learning goals and appropriate pedagogy for those goals. Differences in disciplinary approaches to teaching have been well documented (Donald, 2002; Hativa & Marincovich, 1996) and are also a key factor. Similarly, peer review of the teaching of a graduate teaching assistant, a new part-time faculty member, and an experienced full professor will all take on a different character, particularly in the balance of formative and summative attention given to the review. Institutional context is an additional factor to be noted. As plans are developed and implemented, they must be aligned with the mission and character of the institution and its student demographics, curriculum, and resources.

Central Distinctions in the Evaluation of Teaching Literature

The substantial body of scholarship on the evaluation of teaching includes empirical studies of the validity and reliability of several kinds of evaluation—primarily student ratings, case studies of implementation of programs of teaching evaluation, conceptual work on the assumptions underlying evaluation of teaching, construction of models, and recommendations for practice. For the purposes of this brief review, the focus will be on one distinction central to this literature—the formative-summative distinction—and generally accepted recommendations in the literature.

The Formative-Summative Distinction

Writing within the context of program evaluation, Michael Scriven (1973) introduced two terms, *formative evaluation* and *summative evaluation,* that have become generally adopted for their usefulness in the evaluation of teaching as well. Leading summaries of the state of teacher evaluation, such as the works of Arreola (2007), Braskamp and Ory (1994), Cashin (1996), Centra (1993), Knapper and Cranton, (2001), Paulsen (2002), Ryan (2000), and Seldin and Associates (2006) all contain a discussion of these terms, situating them as critical in defining the goals and use of any evaluation activity.

Formative evaluation. Within the context of teacher evaluation, the term *formative evaluation* describes activities that provide teachers with information that they can use to improve their teaching. The information is intended for their personal use, rather than for public inspection, and thus is private and confidential. The information should be rich in detail so that teachers can obtain clear insights into the nature of their teaching strengths and weaknesses. Often, text comments or a multitude of very specific rating items tied to course goals and practices will be employed to provide this. Information can come from students, colleagues, administrators, or even through self-reflection or systematic data collection by teachers themselves, such as classroom research. Formative evaluation is informal, ongoing, and wide-ranging. It is the basis for the development of effective teaching throughout one's career.

Summative evaluation. In contrast, summative evaluation of teaching focuses on information needed to make a personnel decision—for example, hiring, promotion, tenure, merit pay. Consequently, the information is for public inspection rather than for the individual faculty member. Since it is not intended to provide rich and detailed data for the improvement of teaching, it is often more general and comparative in nature than data for formative evaluation. Often, quantitative information such as results of rating or ranking activities, or summary information such as letters from reviewers, constitutes the basis for summative evaluation. The information should provide comparative information as well, enabling the evaluator to determine the quality of the teaching performance with respect to the performance of other peers. Frequently, then, summative data will include norms for a comparison group or statements testifying to the performance with respect to others in the department, college, or field. The attempt is to judge merit or worth to the institution generally. Summative evaluation, in contrast to formative evaluation, is conducted at given intervals, such as annual or promotion and tenure reviews.

Centra (1993) observes that the critical consideration is actual, rather than intended, use of the information. For example, if data are collected by a teacher for use in shaping a course, but are later submitted as evidence in a promotion and tenure dossier, these should not be thought of as formative. (Unfortunately, however, they are not likely to constitute very useful summative data if they are not global and comparative.) Centra further notes that those who provide formative feedback should not be summative evaluators as well, since the teachers whom they are evaluating will likely be less open and honest with them when they know that these people will later be their judges in a decision-making situation.

Braskamp and Ory (1994) summarize some key terms used in portraying each distinction. With formative evaluation of teaching, they associate the terms *individual, career oriented, improvement, development,* and *commitment.* With summative, on the other hand, they associate the terms *institutional, reward oriented, accountability, administration,* and *control.*

It must be noted that the distinction between formative and summative evaluation is not always as clear in practice as it is in the literature. Most colleges and universities do not operate separate systems for each purpose. Student ratings of instruction, for example, are often used to provide feedback to instructors, but summaries of scores and comparisons of individual instructors with their peers frequently constitute the main evidence for teaching performance presented in promotion and tenure dossiers. Despite advice to the contrary, most institutions find it simply more efficient to use a body of information that is collected for multiple purposes rather than collect two separate types of information. In practice, then, peer reviewers are often using information collected for formative purposes to make summative judgments.

The separation of formative and summative also creates a more rigid distinction than is necessary between efforts intended to be developmental and those aimed toward preserving the overall quality of the faculty workforce. It is not irrational to assume that engaging in a conversation with a peer about overall lack of interest, skill, or knowledge with respect to teaching *should* lead to consideration of whether the individual in question should continue pursuing a faculty career. Nor is it unreasonable to expect that positive information generated through a mentoring relationship might be used to prompt placement of an individual in a choice assignment or the granting of a major salary increase. Bernstein, Jonson, and Smith (2000) suggest using alternating periods of development and evaluation: "If faculty have resources and time for formative peer review that is shielded from scrutiny for periods of a few years, they can generate substantial improvement in teaching that can be brought forward during periodic times of accountability"

(p. 83). In another publication, Bernstein (1996) describes the implementation of a program based on the alternating phases.

In sum, although the formative/summative distinction is helpful in guiding evaluation efforts, in practice it is hard to employ rigidly.

Multiple Sources, Methods, and Points in Time

The evaluation literature has continually stressed that for evaluations of teaching to be fair, valid, and reliable, multiple sources of information must be engaged, multiple methods must be used to gather data, and the data must be gathered over multiple points in time. For example, classroom observations can certainly occur on days that are atypical of what happens in a particular course. The activity may be unusual, such as the one day when student presentations are scheduled. The composition of the students may be different, perhaps due to a long weekend ahead or a contagious illness. The faculty member may be having an off day, or a particularly enthusiastic and focused day. Similarly, results from one course may be unusual because it was the first time it was taught, it was team-taught, or it was challenged by mishaps in room assignment, resources availability, instructional technology problems, or the like. Relying on only one method, such as classroom observation, can yield results that are different from what might be obtained from looking at other data, such as the testing practices of the course. Similarly, using the opinions of one peer rather than a group of peers provides a limited perspective. To counter these threats to the usefulness of peer review, multiple sources, methods, and points in time are needed.

Multiple sources. Scholars make distinctions based on which group is the most informed source on the area of teaching to be evaluated and which kinds of data are likely to be most illuminating for a given purpose.

Instructors being evaluated are the primary source of *descriptive* data in that they are the generators of course materials, the teaching philosophy statement and information on number and kind of courses taught, participation in classroom research, leadership in the department or discipline in the area of teaching, thesis and dissertation supervision, mentoring of graduate teachers, and other pertinent descriptions.

Colleagues who are serving as evaluators are best suited to provide *judgmental* response on a person's subject matter expertise, the currency and appropriateness of their teaching materials, their assessment approaches, professional and ethical behavior, and the like. In the role of mentor, colleagues provide feedback in constructive ways; as summative evaluators, they make decisions about the comparative quality of the person being evaluated.

Administrators, particularly the department chairperson, can corroborate or supplement descriptions of teaching contributions to the department and to the profession, of professional ethics, thesis or dissertation supervision, the mentoring of graduate teachers, and the like. They can also evaluate the quality of these factors, compared with other faculty in the unit.

Students provide the primary judgmental data about the quality of the teaching strategies employed in courses and their assessment of the personal impact of the teacher on their learning. They can also corroborate or supplement the descriptive data made by the instructor.

Multiple methods. Among the methods available for providing evaluative information are the soliciting of narrative documents from any of the above sources (such as the request to prepare a teaching portfolio or letter of recommendation), inspection of materials (such as syllabi, tests, or portfolios), rating or ranking forms (such as student ratings or classroom observation checklists), observations of teaching or committee work performance, counts (such as number of student theses supervised), and telephone or in-person interviews.

Multiple points in time. Given its nature, formative evaluation should be ongoing; thus, these activities should be continual over the instructor's career. For summative evaluation, a systematic schedule outlining when given types of evidence will be collected should be set up, ensuring that a reasonable sampling over the time period being evaluated will be obtained.

Ways in Which Peer Review of Teaching Is Used

As noted at the beginning of this chapter, peer review of teaching is implicit in many activities that regularly take place in colleges and universities. Under the best circumstances, these activities are based on some consensus about what constitutes teaching excellence and on providing those conducting the reviews with good evidence on which to base their judgments. The principle of *constructive alignment* coined by John Biggs (2003) might be extended to peer review. Speaking of alignment between intended learner outcomes, activities, and assessment methods, Biggs advocates that these elements of education be aligned. The application to faculty teaching would imply that identification of the teaching practice we wish to see should be aligned with the ways in which we try to develop teaching and the ways in which we assess it.

A thoughtful articulation of institutional values for teaching and characteristics of effective teaching within its context is the important basis for any teaching evaluation activity. When faculty members are hired; when they are judged for merit increases, promotion, or tenure; when they are considered for teaching awards; or when they undergo post-tenure review, this statement of values should frame the discussion. When evidence displaying the performance of particular members of the faculty is collected, it should be aligned with the particular qualities, knowledge, and performance that are valued. Forms and checklists for reviewing classroom performance or teaching materials, candidate statements, or portfolio systems that serve as evidence can be used for several different purposes. And teaching development efforts should be informed by this framework as well. Ways in which peer review of teaching has been used vary from one institution to the next. Some examples follow.

Hiring Decisions

Almost all institutions use peer review of teaching as part of their employment process. When a candidate is asked to supply teaching materials, such as syllabi, to teach a demonstration class, or to produce a philosophy of teaching statement, these forms of evidence should be assessed according to the criteria and standards for good teaching at the institution, possibly even including some of the same instruments or processes used to assess teaching for other purposes. Perlman and McCann (1996) outline such an approach, providing advice on how to prepare search committee members to evaluate the teaching of potential candidates. Shulman (1996, 2005) advocates the pedagogical colloquium, a forum for exploration of the ideas of the candidate on teaching practice, as a way to determine the candidate's fit for the faculty position and as an occasion for an exchange about practice between existing faculty.

Communities of Practice

Wenger (1999) and Wenger, McDermott, and Snyder (2002) have discussed the establishment of a *community of practice* in professional settings—groups of colleagues united by an interest in a common question or set of questions about their practice, who gather to address these. Several recent national projects involving peer review of teaching might be classified as communities of practice. For example, in the former American Association for Higher Education's Peer Review of Teaching Project, several of the exercises participants used, such as reflecting with others on a critical moment in their teaching, were designed to promote group inquiry on teaching (these exercises can be found in Hutchings, 1995). The Peer Review of Teaching Project at the University of Nebraska, based on the exchange of course portfolios, was designed for the same purpose (Bernstein, 2002; Bernstein, Burnett, Goodburn, & Savory, 2006; University of Nebraska, n.d.).

The faculty learning community model originating at Miami University (Cox & Richlin, 2004) has promoted such reflective gatherings on individual teaching issues as well as general questions of teaching practice. While all three projects involved peer review of individuals in that they provided formative feedback to the individual participants, they situated this activity in a collegial setting, expanding the individual issues into common topics for inquiry.

In like manner, teaching circles—groups of faculty who gather to discuss common issues of practice—also inevitably involve a subtle kind of formative feedback to their members. Maintaining a departmental syllabus or teaching materials file, which is used for reflection and commentary on practice, is also a form of peer review. Peer review for institutional improvement purposes has become commonplace in British institutions as a result of national leadership on the improvement and professionalization of teaching. Hammersley-Fletcher and Orsmond (2004) describe the positive reception of this approach and the ways it has been implemented.

COACHING FACULTY

Programs for formative use of peer review of teaching abound. Many are described in Quinlan (1996). The assignment of a mentor to new faculty is a common example. In these mentoring programs, some more formal than others, the senior partner establishes a relationship with the new faculty member, observing teaching performance, helping with the production of teaching materials, and generally assisting with teaching dilemmas. Sometimes, creative approaches are used in these mentoring pairs, such as grading papers from each other's class and comparing results or "taking" each other's course for a short period, including completing the assignments, to gain a student perspective. In many cases, colleges and universities have teaching and learning centers where professional staff members are available to observe classes, comment on materials, discuss assumptions and theories, gather student feedback, and coach faculty. These centers often use standard approaches or protocols, and their consultants are trained in the collection of data on teaching and on providing constructive feedback. The teaching centers listed on such sites as that maintained by the University of Kansas (www.ku.edu/%7Ecte/resources/websites.html) often describe these services on their web pages.

Reciprocal peer review of teaching pairs or teams is used at many institutions. Elbow (1980) provides a classic portrait of one such arrangement, based on exchange of letters. Handal (1999) describes a system of "critical friends." Katz and Henry (1988) talk about an approach that became the basis for the New Jersey Master Teacher Program, which was adopted by several colleges and institutions in New Jersey and elsewhere. In this approach, teachers administer a survey to their students, make reciprocal classroom visits, and jointly discuss the results. For descriptions of how some other institutions use peer review of teaching formatively, see the web sites of the University of Wisconsin–Madison (http://teachingacademy.wisc.edu/Assistance/MOO/index.htm), North Carolina State University (www.ncsu.edu/provost/peer_review/), and the University of Minnesota (www1.umn.edu/ohr/teachlearn/resources/peer/index.html).

REVIEWING FACULTY FOR SALARY INCREASES, CONTRACT RENEWALS, AND PERFORMING ANNUAL REVIEWS

Depending on the pattern of administration, and usually the size of an academic unit, peer review may be involved in the evaluation of yearly performance of teaching (as well as other roles) of faculty members. While the unit administrator might do these reviews independently in some cases, in others a committee of peers is involved. Once again, such processes benefit from alignment with the institution's professed values on teaching and the criteria and standards articulated for effective performance. These may be locally adapted for specific teaching contexts. The types of evidence that faculty offer to show their performance relative to these standards should be carefully enumerated. More and more institutions are using technology, such as faculty electronic portfolios, for the collection of this information. ("Electronic portfolios," 2005; Barrett, 2001; Walcerz, 1999; Woodroof & Searcy, 2004). The capability of the traditional paper annual review form can be enhanced by allowing for the inclusion of artifacts such as attachments of papers emanating from the scholarship of teaching, sample student products, and the like. Reviewers can drill down in the information stack to get a deeper sense of the faculty member's performance. By serving as a storage vehicle for past accomplishments and such foundational documents as teaching philosophy statements, eportfolios can provide a retrospective look and allow new evidence to be viewed in the context of the development pattern. The use of faculty eportfolios can also promote efficiency, in that they constitute a cumulative database that can be searched within an individual case or across cases when information is sought, saving the faculty member or unit administrator from compiling the same information repeatedly in different forms.

DETERMINING FACULTY ASSIGNMENTS

Unit administrators or colleagues, such as course leaders, may use peer review of teaching to make decisions on teaching assignments. Determining which faculty member will teach a critical course, advise honors students, or chair the curriculum committee are instances of decisions that can benefit from systematic peer review. In these cases, very specific attributes may constitute the criteria for the selection. For example, the assignment as honors advisor might require a faculty member who excels at interpersonal rapport with students, exhibits high expectations for student performance, and knows the curriculum well. If this subset of characteristics is part of the overall approach to the collection of information on teaching performance in the unit, faculty assignments can be made in a more evidence-based way than they usually are.

JUDGING PROMOTION AND TENURE CASES

Perhaps the most widespread use of peer review of teaching is the summative activity that takes place in the promotion and tenure process. Almost universally, colleges and universities require the compilation of a faculty dossier for these purposes and the review of this dossier by peers both internal and external to the institution. Criteria and standards for judging teaching performance in these dossiers are sometimes well articulated, but often are rather vague. In many cases, external reviewers are expected to comment mostly on research or service performance, rather than on teaching quality. Internal reviewers frequently rely mostly on student evaluation results and load information to judge teaching. It is in this arena that systematic peer review of teaching can be quite helpful. Not only can a thorough approach to evaluating teaching do justice to the candidates under review, it can send a clear institutional signal about the expectations for teaching performance. For example, at Indiana University–Purdue University Indianapolis, faculty who wish to demonstrate excellence in teaching must meet criteria that include evidence of publicly disseminated scholarship of teaching and learning. This is a powerful message to faculty about institutional values. (To view the teaching dossier criteria of this institution, access the statement at http://www.opd.iupui.edu/uploads/library/APPD/APPD6355.pdf.)

APPROVING TEACHING SABBATICAL REQUESTS

Whether conducted by a college or university committee, a committee within the academic unit, or by an administrator, the approval process for requests for sabbaticals pertaining to teaching development is also an occasion for peer review. Although sabbaticals are usually devoted to conducting disciplinary research, some are aimed toward research on teaching topics, development of new approaches to teaching, and the like. In these cases, the proposal and the faculty applicant's past teaching performance can be examined with the same basic criteria and standards used for other teaching decisions. Does the proposal hold promise for increasing reflective practice? Will it enable deeper learning in students, more authentic assessment, improved use of instructional technology? Modification of forms used for other aspects of peer review of teaching can help reviewers to judge sabbatical requests within the context of overall teaching values.

Choosing Teaching Awards Winners

Similarly, when a teaching awards program is developed, the criteria and standards for the award should be aligned with those that have already been institutionally announced. Evidence for judging the extent to which these characteristics are exemplified in the work of specific candidates might be similar to that produced for other purposes. Although the expected achievement of standards may be higher, the evidence need not be of a different type. Sadly, a recent exploration of teaching awards programs (Chism, 2005, 2006) found that very few are based on stated criteria and standards and the match of evidence to these. When peer review for the purpose of making teaching awards is done haphazardly, it undermines the value of the award.

Conducting Post-Tenure Reviews

Although post-tenure reviews often are based on the same process as annual reviews, some special considerations concerning the teaching performance of post-tenure faculty may be noted. There may be more emphasis, for example, on teaching service and leadership, such as mentoring and coaching others or chairing teaching-related committees within the department. Expectations for currency of content and use of innovative approaches to teaching should be maintained. As with all peer review activities, it is important to continue peer review for formative as well as summative purposes for post-tenure faculty.

In short, across the spectrum of faculty activity, peer review can figure in a variety of evaluation activities. Hoyt and Pallett (1999) present a useful chart detailing the checkpoints for evaluation activity over the faculty career that might be consulted for ideas.

Why Use Peer Review?

To traditional calls that have advocated the peer review of teaching, several recent arguments have been added that focus on the responsibility of the profession to monitor itself. Foremost among the recent arguments is the call to make teaching the subject of public discourse and scholarly activity. It is argued that in order for teaching to be valued, it must go beyond the private and personal. When teaching is viewed as professional knowledge, there must be an accepted way to define characteristics of teaching excellence and to make judgments based on a stated set of criteria and standards that reflect the complexity of teaching. Because peer review is a way of making teaching public, it is also seen as enhancing the value of teaching and engaging peers in scholarly examination of their profession.

Teaching as Community Property

The idea of teaching as community property has been promoted vigorously by Lee Shulman of Stanford University through his involvement in a project of the former American

Association for Higher Education called "From Idea to Prototype: The Peer Review of Teaching" (Hutchings, 1994, 1995, 1996a, 1996b). Noting that the culture of teaching in higher education settings has developed a strong norm of privacy, Shulman (1993) points out that such a culture inhibits the growth of what Boyer (1990) has termed the *scholarship of teaching,* the thoughtful, problem-solving, discipline-based approach to teaching that involves continual reasoning about instructional choices, awareness of the solutions that other scholars have made to key problems in facilitating student learning in the field, and active, ongoing research about the effects of instructor actions on student learning.

Those who advance the notion of teaching as community property talk about various kinds of collaborative activity among faculty, such as team teaching, teaching circles (inquiry groups similar to quality circles in corporate settings), the teaching seminar as a routine part of the interview process, and departmental libraries of syllabi, course materials, and research papers on college teaching (Hutchings, 1996a; Quinlan, 1996). They also support a prominent role for peer review of teaching. The rationale is that the faculty must be continually engaged in discussing teaching both to nurture new teachers into the community of teacher-scholars and to render the process of making personnel decisions (who gets hired, who gets tenured, who gets merit pay, and the like) more open and more informed by reasoned decisions that consider teaching seriously. The idea is thus in the spirit of both continuous quality improvement and the practice of self-regulation within professions.

Writing within the context of the initiation of peer review, Ludwick, Dieckman, Herdtner, Dugan, and Roche (1998) observe the benefits of a community of practice:

> A sense of community evolved as faculty dialogued and worked to develop the peer review process. Discussions about common clinical problems and possible solutions provided a sense of cohesiveness. Part-time and full-time, junior and senior faculty members were empowered to disclose problems and to offer solutions and sometimes with the increased use of part-time faculty, distance learning, diverse clinical sites, and increased teaching loads. . . . The task force meetings and clinical peer review process resulted in an increasingly connected and invigorated faculty. (p. 20)

Teaching as a Scholarly Activity

Making teaching a topic for communal discourse addresses the goal of elevating teaching as a form of scholarship. Just as with other forms of scholarship, public examination, debate, and engagement enrich the inquiry. Scholars and policymakers alike now argue that teaching is too important to leave to individual experimentation and private trial-and-error learning, but must benefit from collective dialogue and sharing of successes and discoveries. The argument is that not only will this collective approach be more effective, but also more efficient, as principles of practice are developed and shared with new professionals.

Inquiry about teaching, especially when it is incorporated into meetings of professional associations, professional journals, and other communication vehicles, will encourage far more systematic research into central issues that have remained relatively unexplored: How do students learn to transfer theoretical information on conservation of energy to a specific case? What teaching strategies can facilitate the process? For which learners? As faculty engage in peer review, these questions come to the fore. Their natural intellectual curiosity then turns to issues that can be addressed for their own teaching and for that of their professional colleagues.

An example of the establishment of this community of teaching scholars is the Peer Review of Teaching Project led by the former American Association for Higher Education in the 1990s (Hutchings, 1995) and follow-up projects such as the Peer Review of Teaching Project at the University of Nebraska led by Daniel Bernstein (Bernstein, 2002; University of Nebraska, n.d.). Peer exchange is based on teaching portfolios exchanged among faculty participants. These provide rich occasions for discussions of teaching dilemmas and successes documented in the portfolios, stimulating group reflection and exchange. Similarly, Hammersley-Fletcher and Orsmond (2004) document how the implementation of peer observation of teaching in British institutions has stimulated the growth of a culture of conversation about teaching.

DEVELOPMENTAL POWER

The element of feedback is certainly one of the most important components of any learning process, underscoring a key purpose of peer review—to help teachers improve their practice. As they become aware of aspects of their teaching that are ineffective or identify strengths to build on, they can change their ways of acting accordingly. If, in talking with others, they think of their practice in new ways or learn of other strategies, those under review by peers expand their knowledge of teaching and add to their repertoire of skills.

The adage "to teach is to learn twice" describes an additional feature of peer review related to the above points about community and scholarship. As peers observe others, they learn something about themselves. Peer review has the potential to provide developmental gain not only for the person being reviewed, but also for the reviewer. This point is underscored by Beckman (2004), who observed the impact of a peer review program in a clinical setting on his own practice. Modeling and observing others are key ways for teachers to learn new practices and to self-critique: Growth of the reviewer is thus a natural byproduct of the process of peer review.

CLARIFICATION OF CHARACTERISTICS OF TEACHING EXCELLENCE

Several long-standing observations about the nature of teaching excellence continue to plague efforts to prepare, support, and assess those who teach in higher education. One of these is the claim that teaching is an ephemeral "art," incapable of being analyzed and perhaps inextricably intertwined with personality. Such claims lead to the conclusion that teachers are born, not made, and that attempts to understand teaching are inevitably reductionist and should not be pursued. The opposite claim is that we can define characteristics of teaching with certainty and clarity. Yet a look at the literature on teaching effectiveness (Chism, 2004) shows that most studies present a partial and not uncontested view of these characteristics. The first claim can lead to abandonment of any efforts to study teaching, and the second to systems of evaluation that are inappropriate or incomplete.

It is important, then, that teaching excellence be continually defined in context by peers sensitive to the particulars of the teaching environment and engaged in an activity that requires attention to the nature of expertise. Although general lists of characteristics of effective teaching can be gleaned from the literature, they require interpretation and application to specific settings. Judging whether certain sequencing of content or the use of certain metaphors and examples is helpful can be done most effectively by others who understand the discipline and setting. The development of consensus on signs of effective teaching and ways to measure them requires the kind of dialogue among peers that is inherent in peer review of teaching. The communal dialogue that occurs is likely to increase the understanding of teaching's complexity, generating practical guidelines for assessing teaching owned by the specific teaching community that will use them. Furthermore, when reflections emanating from peer review activity are shared across contexts, the nature of the conversation on characteristics of teaching excellence will be enhanced.

ARGUING FOR THE VALUE OF TEACHING

The value of teaching at colleges and universities has been continually challenged during the past several decades by the association of research activity with both prestige and as the remedy for fiscal shortfalls. In addition, the employment of lower-paid teachers (graduate teaching assistants and part-time temporary faculty) has escalated, freeing up tenure-track faculty to conduct research, further augmenting status distinctions between the relative values of teaching and research.

Higher tuitions, more involved parents, and demands of employers for a more educated citizenry, however, are beginning to push the balance in the opposite direction. Peer review of teaching will be essential in this new concentrated effort to improve teaching and learning. Its actual effect on improvement will clearly be sought, but the use of peer review will also serve a symbolic function of the value that the institution places on quality of teaching. The investment of faculty time, coupled with increased articulation of expectations and standards associated with a good peer review process, are both testimony to value.

An additional force addressing the value issue is the focus on teaching as a scholarly activity. As the nature of teaching becomes the focus of inquiry and shared public dialogue, its relative value as scholarly activity increases. Shulman (1993) argues that only when teaching becomes community property, rather than isolated, individual action, will it be valued. Indeed, many institutions are now expecting faculty to document the scholarship of teaching and learning for promotion and tenure and other considerations. The activities inherent in peer review contribute to dialogue on teaching as a scholarly act.

ACKNOWLEDGING APPROPRIATE COMPLEXITY

The importance of the teaching mission to the institution, the situational nature of teaching, and the complex web of instructional decisions and effects involved in teaching lead to another argument for peer review of teaching: that any good approach to evaluating teaching will reflect the complexity of teaching itself. Over the years, the evaluation of teaching has gone from a very informal and unarticulated process to one that now relies quite heavily on numeric averages from teaching evaluation instruments that are rated by students (Seldin, 1993a). While the inclusion of student ratings has ensured that some data are considered during the process of evaluating teaching, those who study evaluation of teaching are strong in their warnings that the process must rely on multiple sources of evidence from multiple parties (Braskamp & Ory, 1994; Centra, 1993; Stake & Cisneros-Cohernour, 2000).

Specifically, experts indicate that while students are the most appropriate judges of day-to-day teacher behaviors and attitudes in the classroom, they are not the most appropriate judges of the accuracy of course content, use of acceptable teaching strategies in the discipline, and the like. For these kinds of judgments, peers are the most appropriate source of information. Sell and Chism (1988) list the following as areas for which peers are the best source of judgments on teaching performance: subject matter expertise, course goals, instructional materials and methods, assessment and grading practices, student achievement, professional and ethical behavior, and thesis supervision. Shulman (cited in Hutchings, 1995) distinguishes between judging technical and substantive aspects of teaching, arguing that an intelligent outsider can make determinations about the teacher's speaking skills and the like, but that only a peer can judge whether the teacher is dealing with the subject matter in an accurate and responsible fashion.

Batista (1976, p. 269) provides the following list of faculty behaviors that peers are most suited to judge:

1. Up-to-date knowledge of subject matter
2. Quality of research
3. Quality of publications and papers
4. Knowledge of what must be taught
5. Knowledge and application of the most appropriate or most adequate methodology for teaching specific content areas
6. Knowledge and application of adequate evaluative techniques for the objectives of his/her course(s)
7. Professional behavior according to current ethical standards
8. Institutional and community services
9. Personal and professional attributes
10. Attitude toward and commitment to colleagues, students, and the institution

Since a central attribute of professions is the self-monitoring of the quality of performance within the profession rather than reliance on external agencies, peer review of teaching is one way that the professoriate can address this responsibility to uphold standards of the profession.

The recommendation that emerges is for an approach to the evaluation of teaching that mirrors the complexity of teaching itself. The idea of teaching portfolios or dossiers has increasingly become popular, advancing the notion that several types of evidence are important in documenting teaching and that these artifacts make more sense when woven together with a teacher narrative that situates them in the specific context in which they have occurred. Peer review of teaching features prominently in such multidimensional portraits of teaching.

Objections to Peer Review

Even though arguments for peer review of teaching are strong, persistent faculty objections are documented in the literature (Menges, 1991; Pister & Sisson, 1993). These include anxieties about openness and possible threats to academic freedom, the difficulty of defining a peer, problems with finding time to devote to peer review, concerns about the validity and reliability of peer review, and concerns about undesirable aftereffects of the approach.

OPENING THE CLASSROOM DOOR

The norms of privacy that have surrounded teaching in recent times are quite powerful. Most teachers, not only those in higher education, have grown accustomed to making teaching decisions without the advice of others and to conducting classes without being observed by others. Although many have experienced perfunctory visits during their first year or two of teaching, such occasions have not been regular and have generally been viewed as "tests" rather than as opportunities to talk about teaching development. The observer has generally been uncomfortable as well, feeling obligated to visit but also having the sense that privacy is being violated.

Such concerns are quite understandable given the norms that have developed, yet several responses can be made. First, equating peer review only with classroom observation is a mistake. As this sourcebook will detail, classroom observation is only one form of peer review—and the one that has traditionally been found least reliable. Second, successful implementation of peer review requires culture change. Handal (1999) distinguishes between "individual freedom" (to do what I want) and "professional autonomy" (acting within the norms of the professional group), arguing that professionalism in teaching means being knowledgeable about the basis for one's work in the community of one's associates.

If the norm of community does not replace the idea of individual teaching entrepreneurs, norms of privacy and competition will prevail. Within the community culture, talks about teaching are continual, not restricted to the visit. Teaching is viewed as inherently interesting and challenging, so the discussion becomes less a critique of individual performance and more an exchange about strategies for solving complex and intriguing problems. If talk of teaching, review of teaching materials, collaboration on teaching, and visits to colleagues' classes characterize a department, concerns about threats to academic freedom are less likely than in settings in which an individual, competitive culture prevails. Further, Hutchings (1994) points out, "With the right 'prompts,' faculty *want* to talk to colleagues about teaching" (p. 5). In their study of the influence of departmental culture on the ability of faculty to work collaboratively on teaching and learning, Massy, Wilger, and Colbeck (1994) found, "Faculty in departments that support teaching appear to be less intimidated by peer evaluation than their colleagues in other departments" (p. 16). They point out that junior faculty socialized within a system of peer review are less anxious than those "who have worked for a long time in a system where teaching takes place behind closed doors" (p. 17).

A related line of thinking questions the focus of teaching evaluation activity on the individual rather than the community. Although scholars writing about this (Braskamp, 2000; Elton, 1996; Gregory, 1996; Stake & Cisneros-Cohernour, 2000) do not completely argue against evaluation of teaching that focuses on the individual, they stress that the teaching context is a very important influence shaping how teaching and learning are enacted each day. Peer review that does not take this context into effect is thus suspect, and more involvement of the community of teachers in common self-assessment is desired.

WHO IS A PEER?

Over the years, many scholars have wrestled with the question of which colleagues are appropriate peer reviewers. Especially in the case of highly specialized subdisciplines or small departments, it is hard to find a colleague who can provide insights about accuracy and currency of content. For these situations, the best reviewers are likely to be found at another institution, yet the difficulties of distance are then introduced.

Another concern is with the impartiality of peer review, given departmental rivalries and the tendency of human beings to think in terms of their own preferred approach, rather than to value diversity. In an extended analogy, Strenski (1995) compares peer review to the inability of two chefs to agree on the proper way to prepare food. She says, "Ask any instructor about quality of instruction and you will hear an answer inevitably colored by that instructor's own training and model teachers" (p. 34). She cautions that confidence in a peer's opinion must be tempered by knowledge of the philosophical position and pedagogical preferences of the reviewer. Muchinsky (1995) reviews the literature on bias based on friendship and the formation of resulting "mutual admiration societies." He argues that such bias is less likely to occur when peer review is used formatively than when it is used summatively. In addressing both personal and instructional preference biases, judicious assignment of peer review responsibilities becomes quite important.

Miller, Finley, and Vancko (2000) point out that in the 35%–40% of community college campuses that are unionized, department chairs must serve as evaluators since most union contracts do not permit "brothers to evaluate brothers" (p. 55). In these cases, the administrator substitutes for the true peer.

The issues involved in identifying a proper peer are substantial. They are not, however, without parallel in the review of research for publication or funding. While one cannot guarantee impartiality, it seems that the only practical course is to work out issues of bias as they occur, understanding that in the long run, some balance will be achieved if the integrity and health of the profession is to prevail. The involvement of multiple reviewers and continuous cycles in peer review also potentially limits the effect of personal bias. Technology will assist in approaching the problem of distance between reviewers. As course materials are made available through the Internet and classrooms are more frequently televised or become virtual, a reviewer at a distance can readily contribute insights concerning a colleague's instructional decisions.

VULNERABILITY OF THE PEER REVIEWER

A central reason for the reluctance of faculty to serve as peer reviewers—in addition to the personal uneasiness they feel in judging a colleague—is confidentiality. While this is not an issue in formative evaluation, where open and constructive feedback is sought and offered, it becomes quite important when the advancement of a colleague is at stake. While one may expect that professional conduct might encompass having to be open about judgments even when this is personally uncomfortable, such is not always the case. Braskamp (2000) observes, "From my experience, faculty, especially at smaller institutions, are reluctant to judge others. Ironically, the strong relationships and a strong sense of community prevent them from being objective and honest" (p. 30).

Peer reviewers will be more candid, it is argued, when they are sure that their remarks are anonymous. Yet records of reviews where discrimination is suspected are not considered protected, according to a 1991 Supreme Court ruling (*University of Pennsylvania v. EEOC*), and in locations where an open records or sunshine law exists, even more access might be available. One possible way to address concerns emanating from lack of confidentiality is to generate collaborative written records in the name of the entire review committee or to present verbal reports to a summarizer.

Vulnerability is also a consideration when colleagues of different ranks are involved in peer review. Again, the purpose of the review makes a difference. When the focus is on formative evaluation, junior faculty might enjoy and benefit from a mutual exchange in which they comment on another's teaching as well as receive feedback. Involving junior faculty in discussing classroom observations and materials prepared by others engages them in teaching issues and helps them to learn from other colleagues.

The main concern in these instances is the time commitment required of the reviewer. In the case of summative evaluation, most units stipulate that only senior faculty will serve as reviewers. This protects junior faculty time as well as considers their position with respect to power.

No Time

The most frequent and perhaps most difficult hesitation about peer review is the issue of time. Faculty are feeling more time pressures than ever before, and—given their current responsibilities—they view as unrealistic the expectation that they can regularly review others' course materials, write thoughtful and reflective commentaries following class-room visits, and evaluate extensive portfolios.

There are no easy answers to this issue. The most common response acknowledges that peer review will take time, but argues for the priority of this effort, claiming that the importance of teaching to the institutional mission and the effects of instructional deci-sions on the learning of students are too great for evaluation of teaching to be less than thorough. For example, the "Pister Report," which summarizes recommendations on fac-ulty reward in the University of California system, states, "Documentation and evalua-tion of meritorious achievement in teaching require a level of faculty effort well beyond current practice. We urge that peer evaluation of teaching be given the same emphasis now given to peer evaluation of research" (Pister & Sisson, 1993, p. 10).

Others make suggestions for specific time-saving approaches, such as limiting the teach-ing portfolio to succinct, thoughtful statements on selected key issues (Seldin, 2004) or assigning one or two people on a committee to understand a case in depth and present it to others, as is commonly done in grant proposal meetings, rather than asking each member to attend to all portfolios with equal thoroughness (Bernstein, 1996). A third suggestion is to make periodic decisions about the teaching quality of an individual, as is done for publication of research, rather than delaying any decisions for substantial periods of time. At checkpoints, then, faculty can say that they have had X favorable reviews of teaching, much as they can say that they have X publications in refereed jour-nals. The summaries of these reviews, rather than the original materials for the reviews (syllabus and the like), can constitute the evidence in the portfolio. Finally, it is argued that lack of regular peer involvement in formative evaluation is an extravagant waste of time when the result is that ineffective teaching is allowed to continue or faculty are ultimately denied tenure. The tradeoff of investing time to avoid this situation is much more productive.

No Standards

Yet another reservation about peer review is the lack of accepted standards for evaluating teaching. Unlike the review of a paper in which the use of a standard statistical procedure can be assessed for its correctness, the review of teaching seems to many to be based on personal preference alone.

As indicated earlier, the situation is not as fuzzy as some would indicate. Research has isolated effective teaching approaches, yet these are general and rely on professional judgment for application. The models of the decision-making of the courtroom judge or the connoisseur are more appropriate for the judge of teaching performance than the model of the basketball referee with rulebook. The setting of standards is more fluid and more situational than it is for less complex activities, and the application of the standards requires more judgment. It does not follow, however, that judgments will be totally idiosyncratic and biased. And once again, there are clear parallels in the review of research, where standards are often unarticulated. Arreola's work (2007), in particular, contains practical suggestions for defining standards of performance. As has been argued earlier, the very work of setting up systems of peer review of teaching involves thoughtful attention to standards.

Validity and Reliability Issues

Closely related to the concern about standards, especially when peer review is used for the purpose of making personnel decisions, are anxieties about the validity and reliability of peer review. The internal validity question—Are we measuring what we intend to measure?—does rely on some consensus about what good teaching looks like in the specific situation at hand. In addition, however, the internal validity question engages the question of inquiry method. Since recommendations on the implementation of peer review embed the approach within a design that not only involves consensus on standards, but advocates multiple reviewers, multiple methods, and sustained engagement, it can readily be seen that such a system has distinct validity advantages to the single source (student ratings) approach or the "gut feeling" approach.

Concerns about reliability—Are we measuring consistently and accurately?—are supported in the scholarly literature, especially the research on classroom observation. For example, several scholars (Ceci & Peters, 1982; Centra, 1975; Cohen & McKeachie, 1980; Feldman, 1989; Kane & Lawler, 1978) have found that peer reviewers disagreed substantially on their assessments of the same classroom teaching performance. Centra (1994) found a high level of disagreement on judgments of portfolios as well.

The problems appear to be connected to three key factors: lack of consensus on standards for judgment, lack of observation or content analysis skills on the part of the reviewers, and lack of systematic process and documentation. In a later study, Centra (2000) found reliable results for peer review of teaching portfolios when the peer reviewer was not selected by the person being reviewed. He suggests the use of small "Committees on Teaching" elected for three years to review portfolios during that period. Root (1987) also found reliable results were obtained for peer review of portfolios when the conditions of the review (explicit criteria and careful selection and preparation of reviewers) were favorable.

A special caution concerning bias applies to the cases of underrepresented faculty in the peer review process. Whether the issues are gender, race, sexual orientation, or marginalization by discipline or type of approach, the prevailing cultural bias of our society infuses the work of the academy in the same way that it influences other societal institutions. Faculty who stress single authorship or value only quantitative approaches, who disdain advising and mentoring as unimportant work, or who think of some areas of study as fluff are apt to judge those who favor collaboration, qualitative approaches, and student-centered service as low-value activities. It is important that criteria and standards reflect inclusive values to help counteract the "invisible bias of the traditional" that can contaminate the peer review process. All of these issues pertaining to validity and reliability are not insurmountable, but they clearly must be addressed in an implementation plan to ensure the success of peer review.

Undesirable Aftereffects

Some concerns about peer review, especially for promotion and tenure decisions, focus on undesirable outcomes, such as divisiveness within the department. The argument is that confidentiality of the reviewer will be difficult to preserve and the resulting openness will make the reviewer more cautious about negative judgments and the colleague under review more likely to take such judgments personally. While the most long-term response to this fear is that the culture must change to support open, collective inquiry on teaching and thus eliminate the desire for secrecy, the short-term response is that multiple peer reviewers must be involved in any one case. The resulting decision is collectively rendered, rather than the personal judgment of one person.

A second concern is that, when used for decisions about tenure or merit increases, peer review of teaching will reduce risk-taking in teaching: Faculty will use only traditional strategies because they fear that initial failures or adjustments necessary to test innovative techniques will be documented, tainting their review. Initial attempts toward innovative teaching often misfire and require a period of fine-tuning; therefore, judgments of teaching must be sensitive to a developmental pattern that involves cycles of experimentation. In the case of peer review for ongoing improvement purposes, information on this pattern is imperative, but it is also helpful in the case of peer review for personnel decisions. Indeed, it would be difficult to show improvement in teaching unless there is some evidence that undesirable situations have been identified and worked through. Documentation of this process should be an essential part of a teaching portfolio. The absence of any experimentation, similarly, should be cause for concern. Faculty need to understand these expectations of the review process in order to feel comfortable about attempts to innovate.

Third is the apprehension that legal challenges to personnel decisions will increase with the use of peer review of teaching. Since the existing system for evaluating teaching is generally based on student ratings data and peer opinion, there does not seem to be a logical basis that a system that is based on multiple sources and kinds of data, including peer review information, would be more vulnerable than the current system. In fact, when peer review of teaching is implemented systematically, it provides more justification and documentation for a decision.

A good system for the evaluation of teaching that incorporates peer review must address the objections that are raised to the satisfaction of the faculty community. The first step is to invest sufficient effort in setting up a good system, the topic of the following two chapters.

Chapter 2

Setting Up a System for Peer Review

To be effective, peer review of teaching must be situated within a system that emphasizes the value of teaching to the institution and articulates a thoughtful and comprehensive approach to the evaluation of teaching. Developing and implementing such a system requires leadership at each administrative level: institution, college, and department.

Institutional Leadership

A study of faculty and administrator perceptions of the value placed on teaching at major universities found that faculty think administrators place less value on teaching than faculty do (Gray, Diamond, & Adam, 1996). Interestingly, individual faculty members surveyed in this study also think that they place more value on teaching than their colleagues do. In the same survey, administrators said that they place more value on teaching than faculty members perceive them to do. So the picture that emerges is of contrasting perceptions and confused expectations all around. Faculty have a hard time believing administrative pronouncements about the value placed on teaching, and administrators think that faculty themselves are pressuring their colleagues to place less value on teaching than on research. The first step to implementing a peer review of teaching system is clarifying this value question, not only with pronouncements but with actions. In the case of peer review, actions center on requiring documentation of positive peer review for personnel decisions and consistently making judgments based on the total evidence, including peer review.

26

Since teaching is situational, leadership at the institutional level must provide broad guidelines to allow for adaptation at other levels. Among the principles that can be enunciated are:

- Evaluation of teaching must be done in a systematic, thoughtful manner.
- Provisions must be made for both formative evaluation (for improvement) and summative evaluation (for personnel decisions).
- Evaluation of teaching for personnel decisions must be multidimensional and include evidence from multiple sources (the faculty member, students, peers, and relevant others) and multiple kinds of evidence (ratings, reflective statements, narrative appraisals, artifacts of teaching such as syllabi) that occur over an extended period of time. The submitted evidence must indicate the context of the teaching and comparative information on expectations for faculty teaching in the field.
- Evaluation of teaching must be appropriate to the teaching context, and clear guidelines must be accessible to all. Academic units must invest time in developing and announcing their approach to evaluation of teaching and the place of peer review within that system. A written document describing that system should be on file at the institutional level as well as at the level of the academic unit.

Richlin and Manning (1995a) note that systems must also be 1) safe, in that they must ensure that outcomes will not be arbitrary; 2) manageable, given the resources of the unit; and 3) compliant with environmental demands for accountability and quality as well as internal unit needs.

At the institutional level, oversight should be exercised, focused on ensuring that academic units develop and document systems for the evaluation of teaching that are in keeping with these principles. If a system of peer review of teaching is developed at the institutional level, it should be very broad, allowing for adaptation to local circumstances and differences among disciplines.

Resources, such as expert help for academic units developing a system, should also be provided from the institutional level.

College, School, and Division Leadership

In situations where there is a college or school or division structure under the institutional level, it is incumbent on administrators at this level to reinforce the principles and help departments and programs adapt them to their particular teaching situations. When personnel reviews are conducted at this level, it is also important for reviewers to operate within a framework that is consistent with announced values and principles for evaluation. Colleges, schools, and divisions can also provide leadership for formative activities, including mentoring programs, classroom feedback services, and various kinds of teaching discussions. If a system of peer review of teaching is implemented at this level, it must provide for variation across the departments and programs within the college, school, or division.

Departmental Leadership

Much of the work supporting the development of an evaluation of teaching system that includes peer review needs to occur at the department level. The articulated institutional value on teaching is operationalized within the department. If resources and rewards are not allocated in appropriate proportion to the value on teaching, the discrepancy will undermine any pronouncements and documentation. It may help to appoint a strong teaching committee to ensure that decision-making remains consistent with principles. If the department is working within a system of peer review articulated at the institutional or college levels, the task will be adapting the system to the needs of its context and discipline. For example, an occupational therapy department may need to develop additional provisions for evaluation of teaching in clinical practicum settings. A physics department may need to insert questions on laboratory instruction into a more general classroom observation guide.

Assessing Readiness for Developing a Peer Review of Teaching System

Often, peer review of teaching activity is implemented in response to an external driver. A new provost requests that units create peer review plans, an external accrediting agency recommends development of a system, a professional association invites the institution to participate in a peer review project, or an event or series of events such as faculty misconduct toward teaching or dissatisfaction with the student evaluation of instruction system triggers interest in peer review. Less frequently, academic units or entire institutions decide themselves that peer review of teaching will help them to achieve their mission.

In any case, one of the first steps involved in developing a peer review plan is to gauge faculty readiness for this initiative. Figure 2.1 outlines an instrument that can be adapted for this use. Based on the most frequent arguments for and against peer review of teaching, the figure will familiarize those assigned with development responsibilities with the arguments needing attention as they begin their work.

Figure 2.1 Assessment of Reception for Implementing Peer Review of Teaching

Rate the extent to which you think these arguments are compelling to your faculty overall.

4 = Especially compelling
3 = Somewhat compelling
2 = Not very compelling
1 = Not at all compelling

Rationale for Peer Review

_____ Professional responsibility argument: As professionals, it is our responsibility to maintain and oversee standards of practice in the work of our colleagues.

_____ Reward argument: Teaching won't be rewarded properly until it is subject to inspection by peers, just as research is. Peer review will raise the status of teaching.

_____ Development of standards argument: Initiating peer review of teaching will result in the articulation of standards of practice, which we have not had before now.

_____ Faculty expectations argument: Having a peer review of teaching program in place will help all faculty to know expectations and get feedback on their performance.

_____ Motivation argument: Making teaching public through subjecting it to peer review will encourage faculty to put more energy into their teaching.

_____ Accountability argument: Peer review of teaching will help satisfy public demands for accountability in higher education.

_____ Mandate argument: Peer review is being mandated across colleges. We have to come up with something we can live with.

_____ Evaluation improvement argument: Thorough evaluation of teaching requires multiple viewpoints (students, peers, self). Our present system of relying mostly on student opinion to judge teaching is unacceptable: Peer review will increase its fairness. Peers are the best source for judging such things as the accuracy and currency of course content.

Total score for strength of rationales: _____

Reservations About Peer Review

_____ It is too hard to define a peer. Specialization, small numbers of faculty in a unit, differences in rank, personality factors, all get in the way of finding appropriate parties for good peer review.

continued on next page

Figure 2.1 *continued*

_____ Peer reviewers are too vulnerable. Legal issues and political repercussions within the academic unit can inhibit the potential for a peer reviewer to be honest.

_____ There is no time to add peer review responsibilities to what faculty are already doing.

_____ There are no standards for good teaching, so peer review is too subjective. Faculty don't really know how to judge teaching.

_____ Teaching is not valued anyway, so investing in peer review is wasteful.

_____ Peer review is being foisted on us.

_____ Our present system of evaluation of teaching works fine without changing the way in which we approach peer review of teaching.

_____ It is awkward for faculty to judge their colleagues' teaching. Teaching seems private and faculty don't like to set themselves up as knowing more about teaching than their peers do.

_____ If peers review teaching, those under review will be afraid to experiment or take risks.

Total score for strength of reservations: _____

Strength of rationales – strength of reservations = _____

Ways of strengthening rationales:

Ways of addressing reservations:

Developing a Statement

Before formulating a plan, it is important to think through the issues that must be considered. In developing a system for the evaluation of teaching, particularly one that includes provisions for peer review, the ideal starting place is an extended and serious conversation in the academic unit that addresses the following questions (sets of questions are also contained in Hutchings, 1995, and Richlin & Manning, 1995b):

1. Who can benefit from evaluation of teaching in this department? (Should it be restricted to pre-tenure faculty, or should senior faculty be included as well?)
2. How do we view the relation between the two purposes of evaluation? (Improvement purposes versus documentation for personnel decisions such as merit increases, promotion, and tenure?) Should we set up separate systems or blend them?
3. What areas of teaching will we assess?
4. How specific can we be in articulating our standards in such areas as:
    - Effective course design
    - Effective classroom performance
    - Effective course materials (syllabi, handouts, tests, coursepacks)
    - Effective contributions to teaching within the department
    - Effective contributions to teaching in the discipline
5. What recommendations will we make on procedures for collecting evidence for those areas of teaching performance that we want to assess?
6. How will we provide resources to accomplish systematic evaluation of teaching?
7. How will we document and communicate our plan?
8. How will we monitor our plan?
9. How often should we revise our plan?

Such a conversation cannot take place in one sitting. Depending on the situation within the academic unit, the leader might appoint a committee to hold preliminary discussions and bring recommendations to others, or small task groups can be assigned responsibility for exploring certain questions and making recommendations for those areas. Eventually, however, a discussion involving all members of the unit should be held, not only to seek input but also to build ownership. Since evaluation of teaching is a sensitive issue, employing a facilitator from another academic unit or someone outside the academic structure might be helpful. The discussions have the potential for initiating critical reflections on teaching that are developmental in themselves and will help to establish the idea of teaching as community property.

Although he notes that there is often resistance, Arreola (2007) observes that the time committed to initial planning will reap results in the efficiency and effectiveness of the process later. He points out that if a major, thoughtful discussion results in clear, accepted standards, applying those standards to particular cases later is not a daunting or mysterious task. The raw materials on which the review is based will not need to be reviewed again at subsequent levels, when the first-level peer review results can be used instead, with considerable reduction in amount of documentation.

The resources that follow in this sourcebook might be a helpful starting point for planning a system of peer review. Chapter 3 outlines in some detail the particular components of such a plan. The forms in the resources section are examples of tools that might be offered to faculty reviewers as part of the system. The forms should be adapted and modified as faculty members see fit to reflect standards appropriate for the field and methods of evaluation most useful in assessing teaching. If the resources provoke considerable dissension, however, it might be best to start with a blank slate and generate standards from the group. Millis (2006) provides ideas on ways in which a faculty group can develop forms for observation of teaching, one component of the process.

The main goal of the process is to develop a clear statement of how teaching will be evaluated within the academic unit, both formatively and summatively. (Two examples of statements are included in this chapter.) Such a system should not be so perfunctory that it does not reflect the complexity of teaching, but it must be realistic in the amount of effort and expertise that its use demands. It must also be consistent with the principles articulated at other levels of the institution.

The statement should be practical. It should be accompanied by resources such as checklists or examples of a good narrative statement evaluating course materials and the like. It should contain how-to advice as well as principles. Particularly in the area of peer review, few resources have been developed in the past, and the process has remained mysterious and idiosyncratic.

If faculty have been involved in developing the academic unit's approach to the evaluation of teaching, obtaining consensus on the final plan should not be difficult. If the large size of an academic unit or the process used to arrive at a plan has precluded broad involvement, a final step in arriving at a plan is to make sure that faculty understand the plan and support it. An additional stage of dissemination, discussion, and modification might be necessary. This is particularly true if a plan is developed at the institutional level.

Finally, the statement and accompanying resources should be disseminated within the academic unit and placed on file at higher institutional levels.

IMPLEMENTING THE SYSTEM

Once the plan has been communicated and has faculty support, it is necessary to determine how to support its accomplishment, monitor progress and problems, and revise it as necessary. In small academic units, the leader might be able to assume these responsibilities and achieve them informally. In larger units, an oversight committee might be assigned responsibility to assess implementation.

Preparing colleagues. One of the most overlooked aspects of incorporating peer review into the evaluation of teaching is preparing colleagues to assess each other's teaching. Paying explicit attention to this aspect at the start will reap rewards as the process unfolds. Organizing sessions to practice with checklists or calibrate by discussing how each would rate a given course material will help faculty to raise questions and understand how to approach this kind of assessment. Practicing giving formative feedback to colleagues in helpful ways can enhance its effectiveness. Reviewing sample materials or videotapes of classroom teaching can stimulate discussion among faculty on how to apply the standards that have been developed and how to use the resources that have been designed. Often, such sessions can be facilitated by a teaching consultant, a skilled member of the department, or a faculty member from another department. Making it clear that part of the assessment of teaching is assessing one's contributions as a peer reviewer will help to reinforce the investment made in developing one's skills.

Distributing responsibilities. In the particular case of peer review, the distribution of responsibilities might be an issue. Assigning colleagues to provide feedback for improvement and to document teaching performance for personnel decisions must be done carefully so that appropriate and helpful assignments are made and time demands are shared equitably. Often a handful of faculty members most skilled in this area are asked to shoulder a disproportionate share of the time commitment. These individuals might be asked to help other faculty learn to become skilled developers of faculty talent as well. Inevitably, the question of conflict of responsibilities between a peer who is assigned both formative and summative functions occurs. In the best of circumstances, the formative and summative information should flow together: Information on what improvements are needed can be tracked to show improvement. Most parties, however, prefer to separate these functions so that the mentor is not the judge. Arrangements for accomplishing this division of responsibilities will need to be made, often by using peers outside the department. Muchinsky (1995) and others observe that when content is being judged, it is best to choose peer reviewers based on knowledge of the discipline, but when general teaching performance is being assessed, it is appropriate, perhaps even desirable, that the reviewers be unfamiliar with the subject so that they can make an assessment based on the role of the naive learner. Others maintain that teaching methods are inextricably intertwined with content and thus only those within the disciplinary specialty can serve as adequate peers. When peers outside the unit are used, they need to understand the context and logistics of the evaluation system as well.

Monitoring the process. Monitoring the thoroughness, timeliness, and fairness of the system will also be important. At the time of annual reviews, it should be clear whether the appropriate activities and their documentation are occurring. The chair or oversight committee can monitor the situation and call for change. If the situation warrants it, the department can be asked to consider changes or to help troubleshoot the situation. Provisions should be made for periodic reexamination of the evaluation of teaching plan and for its revision.

Academic units should be vigilant in examining the process for bias toward underrepresented faculty. Often, gender, race, ethnicity, or other differences, such as working in marginalized fields or in ways that are not always valued (interdisciplinary teaching, team teaching, introductory teaching) surface as contaminating considerations in the peer review process. In many cases, the taken-for-granted assumptions of the reviewers are the issue, but structural bias may exist in the instruments or processes used for decision-making. It is important to educate reviewers as well as developers of peer review systems about such bias. Moody (2005) lists a series of what she terms *cognitive errors* that should be avoided in faculty evaluation. The National Science Foundation has supported projects like ADEPT, the Awareness of Decisions in Evaluating Promotion and Tenure, at Georgia Institute of Technology to help reviewers understand and avoid such bias. The project has produced self-assessment questionnaires, training materials, and a bibliography of resources (see www.adept.gatech .edu/index.htm).

Additional discussions of the development and implementation of peer review systems for both formative and summative purposes are contained in Bernstein (1996); Bernstein, Burnett, Goodburn, & Savory (2006); Hutchings (1996a); and Quinlan (1996). Workbooks for devising systems have been developed by the former American Association for Higher Education (Hutchings, 1995) and Richlin & Manning (1995b).

Example of a Statement

In his discussion of the case of one department's experience in developing and implementing a peer review system, Nordstrom (1995) includes the statement that resulted.

A Protocol for a Peer Review Program in the Department of Marine and Coastal Sciences at Rutgers University

1. The department should have an established process of peer review for faculty to use in improving their course instruction and enhancing their chances of success in personnel decisions.

2. Peer review is strongly recommended, but not required, for all courses an instructor teaches.

3. Peer review should be considered only one of many different ways that teaching effectiveness can be evaluated.

4. The emphasis on peer review should be on its value to the instructor, the process should be instructor-driven, and the results should be the property of the instructor.

5. The review should involve using standardized, faculty-approved worksheets: one for review of course materials and one for review of classroom instruction.

6. The worksheets should be constructed so the reviewers can obtain insight along with the instructor being reviewed.

7. Prompts may be included in the worksheets to ensure that the instructor and the reviewers consider important aspects of a teaching program.

8. The worksheets should be updated periodically to reflect changing departmental goals and conceptions of student learning and to make them compatible with new initiatives for improving teaching effectiveness.

9. The review should be conducted no earlier than midterm if the course is being offered for the first time.

10. The instructor should provide copies of the syllabus and all handouts, assignments, and exams for the review of course materials. A copy of the documentation used for course approval and the description of the course in the university catalog should also be available.

11. At least two in-class observations are suggested for review of classroom instruction.

12. A meeting to discuss teaching issues of mutual interest should be held as part of both the review of course materials and the review of classroom instruction. The meetings also allow the instructor to elaborate on teaching goals and strategies and to rebut negative comments.

13. If the review is to be used in making a personnel decision, the comments on the reviewers' worksheets should be finalized only after these meetings.

14. Use of peer review results in making a personnel decision should occur via the instructor to the maximum extent possible (e.g., through incorporation into a teaching portfolio).

15. Peer reviews for personnel decisions and course improvement should not be conducted simultaneously, but the same reviewer worksheets should be used for both types of review.

16. An individual conducting a review for a personnel decision should have experience in reviewing other courses, should have taught a course at the same level as the course being reviewed, and should be open to alternative teaching strategies and conceptions of student learning.

17. The opportunity for remedial action, through subsequent reviews initiated by the instructor, must be made available following negative reviews made for a personnel decision.

18. Subject to approval by instructors, worksheets may be synthesized to identify department-wide teaching and curricular problems needing remediation.

19. A departmental library of teaching resources should be maintained for faculty use.

The text of another peer review system, this one from the University of Saskatchewan (2003), is reprinted as Appendix A in abbreviated form. This is an example of a comprehensive statement that carefully lays out the rationale and ties it to other university documents, specifies policy with some allowance for adaptation at the local level, and provides for preparation of reviewers and continual development of policy. The original text is linked with sample forms that can be used in the process.

Common Pitfalls to Avoid in Developing and Implementing Peer Review of Teaching Systems

Unfortunately, peer review of teaching has been plagued by a history of stop and start efforts. Ambitious plans are generated but implementation falls short of the mark. Plans meet with strong faculty resistance and are thwarted or shelved. The causes for failure are context-specific, but in general there are some reasons that should be listed as problems to avoid. These include:

- *Ignoring history of poorly done reviews.* In situations where peer review of teaching has been performed in haphazard and uninformed ways, such as the slapdash and noncommittal report following a brief classroom visit by a colleague, it will be necessary to broaden the notion of peer review before faculty will regard the plan as meaningful and worthy of their attention and effort. If their mental model of peer review of teaching is not challenged, it will be hard to involve faculty in the development of a plan or enlist them in using it.

- *No plan, poor plan, overambitious plan.* If peer review is required without any guidance for the reviewers or plan for peer review, efforts are doomed to fail. The results will be idiosyncratic to those doing the reviews and will largely be inconsistent, generating resentment and resistance. Similarly, if there is a plan and it is not well developed or is unrealistic with respect to the commitment and skills of the reviewers, it will likely fail.

- *Lack of buy-in by faculty and/or administrators.* Even a good plan can meet with an untimely death if it is not embraced by the faculty and administrators. Support is needed at both levels. Occasionally, zealous faculty members bring ideas for peer review from their previous institutions, readings, or professional meetings. While their enthusiasm may ignite some of their colleagues, these systems often last for only the life of the faculty member's leadership. Similarly, if an administrator is inspired to support peer review and fails to get faculty on board with the idea, the system will be subverted or will die as the administrator's vigilance is transferred to other projects.

- *Not integrated into other performance systems (promotion and tenure, annual report, awards).* Peer review of teaching systems that are standalone efforts, not aligned with other activities requiring teaching evaluation, face an uphill battle. Although there should be tremendous intrinsic interest in receiving good feedback on teaching, this is not usually the case. It is also not often that the time it takes to do good evaluation is sufficient for completely different evaluations to be done for different purposes. For example, a thorough review of teaching performance and materials that results in a narrative report can also be the basis for an annual review, to be later inserted into a promotion and tenure dossier, and used as an attachment to a teaching award nomination. If separate forms and processes are required for each of these purposes, the system stands a greater chance of falling into disuse.

- *Lack of model for reviewers.* When peer review of teaching plans are couched in generalities, faculty often find it hard to implement them. While it is important that any plan not be so specific that variations in teaching context and individual approaches cannot be accommodated, it is also important to provide concrete examples, forms, or other information that will help faculty to operationalize the plan.

Characteristics of an Effective Peer Review Process

Speaking of evaluation generally, Seldin (2006) enumerated the qualities of a good faculty performance evaluation system as practicality, relevance, comprehensiveness, sensitivity, freedom from contamination, reliability, and acceptability. In his study of the implementation of a system of formative peer review of teaching at a liberal arts college, Keig (2000) made the following recommendations for successful implementation: the improvement purpose of peer review should be stressed; administrators should provide resources for peer review; peer review should focus on more than just classroom performance; systems should provide preparation for reviewers on both reviewing and feedback techniques; faculty should be involved in developing systems of peer review; and faculty who understand the positive power of peer review should be enlisted to "sell" the program.

In summary, the following are characteristics of an effective peer review process:

- It provides for both formative feedback and summative decision-making.
- The process and instrumentation have been developed with attention to thoroughness and fairness.
- Peer reviewers understand their task and are well prepared to accomplish it.
- Trust and confidence in the process is exhibited by all parties.
- Ongoing efforts in the academic unit are invested in improving the peer review process.
- Peer review assignments are made in ways that are likely to result in helpful collaborations.
- Peer review is a valued process within the academic unit.
- Parties are cooperative and timely in accomplishing peer review tasks.

APPENDIX A

Excerpts from the Peer Review of Teaching Statement Developed by the Instructional Development Committee of Council, University of Saskatchewan

Framework for Peer Evaluation of Teaching at the University of Saskatchewan: Best Practices
Approved by University Council June 19, 2003

Author's note: A PDF of resources to be used is attached to the original statement. This excerpt excludes the citations made to the scholarly literature in the original document as support for the policy. These can be seen on the full version at www.usask.ca/university_council/idcc/reports/06-19-03.shtml. Other omissions are indicated by ellipses or noted in brackets.

This framework document should be read in conjunction with the University Council's document entitled *Principles of Evaluation of Teaching at the University of Saskatchewan* approved in March 2002. Units are encouraged to adopt these practices into their evaluation processes over time.

Philosophy

One of the goals of the University, as set out in *A Framework for Planning at the University of Saskatchewan,* is to improve the quality of instructional programs. The Framework document states that the University must be governed by considerations of quality and accountability. "A university that is quality conscious will be accountable to its students, its alumni and the people of the Province" (1998, p. 5). Strengthening the teaching evaluation processes over time will demonstrate the University's concern for quality instruction. By making the evaluation of teaching a more regular process of our teaching activities, the University will be more accountable to students and teachers alike. As the University strives for excellence based on international standards, it is important to gather information about our outstanding contributions to teaching.

University Council's Principles of Evaluation of Teaching at the University of Saskatchewan states "the evaluation of teaching at the University of Saskatchewan may serve several functions. Most importantly, teaching evaluations are to be used to assist faculty with the development and improvement of instruction. Data collected from teaching evaluations can also serve a summative function to assist with collegial and administrative decisions" (University of Saskatchewan, 2002, p. 4).

The University of Saskatchewan Standards for Promotion and Tenure establishes that "good teaching is expected of all faculty and evaluation of teaching...requires more than classroom performance. Candidates will be expected to demonstrate mastery of their subject area(s) or discipline(s), to make thorough preparation for their classes, to communicate effectively with their students, to show a willingness to respond to students' questions and concerns, and to exhibit fairness in evaluating students....faculty are expected to remain committed to improving/enhancing their teaching performance and to remedy problems identified with their teaching. As faculty progress through the ranks, they will be expected to extend their knowledge of their field(s) or discipline(s), i.e., with respect to classes, currency of the material presented, and new teaching methods" (University of Saskatchewan, 2002, http://www.usask.ca/vpacademic/collegial/university_StandardsFeb122002.shtml#D2). In addition, we advocate that faculty should consistently consider and employ effective teaching methods.

The University of Saskatchewan appreciates the commitment of sessional lecturers to good teaching. Teaching evaluations may be conducted for consideration of right of first refusal for sessional lecturers. Peer evaluations must be consistent with the procedures set out in Articles 14—Right of First Refusal—and 18—Formal Teaching Assessment of the Collective Agreement between the University of Saskatchewan and CUPE 3287.

Commitment to high quality instruction and improvement of instruction is the responsibility of all engaged in instructional activities. Instructors should strive to achieve excellence in teaching and to explore best practices for student learning.

Peer Consultation

It is important to understand the difference between peer consultation and peer evaluation of teaching. Peer consultation is a process initiated at the request of the teacher as a way to gather feedback about their teaching. Often this type of peer coaching is non-evaluative and non-judgmental; it is based on classroom observation and/or a review of teaching materials followed by feedback on ways to improve specific instructional techniques.... By contrast, formal peer evaluation is a process initiated by the Department Head or the Dean of a non-departmentalized college for the purpose of gathering information needed for collegial decision-making processes including renewal of probation, tenure, promotion, salary review, right of first refusal and for the review of academic programs.

For purposes of peer consultation, the Gwenna Moss Teaching and Learning Centre offers a Peer Consultation Programme for teachers, although teachers can initiate a consultation on their own. Peer consultants are not chosen from the client's department or non-departmentalized college. The Programme at the Teaching and Learning Centre is voluntary, collaborative and confidential in nature. Teachers may request a consultation for many reasons:

1. To obtain feedback on changes they have made in a course;
2. To discover what's going well;
3. To improve their overall teaching skills or address a particular concern; and,
4. To discuss ideas and innovations with a peer

Peer Evaluation

Peer evaluations are an important aspect of the review of teaching and teaching performance.... Peer evaluation of teaching can be both formative and summative. Peer evaluators of teaching are expected to share feedback to improve teaching (formative) and to provide an evaluation of teaching for use in administrative or collegial decisions (summative). This document will focus on summative peer evaluations.

a) Formative Evaluation

Information gathered from the proper evaluation of teaching may be used for formative purposes to assist with instructional development and improvement.... Informal formative peer evaluations and comments from classroom observations can assist faculty in their development as teachers. Formative techniques of evaluation can also help teachers assess their success with trying new teaching approaches or techniques in the classroom.... Formative peer evaluations may include video-taping lectures and reviewing them with a more experienced teacher to determine ways to improve in the classroom. Another example of formative peer evaluation may include working with small groups of teachers or with a mentor to share information and insight on teaching. There can be great value from the interaction between teacher and reviewer as the reviewer can also learn through the process. Departments and colleges are encouraged to support this experiential approach to instructional development.

b) Summative Evaluation

For summative purposes, evaluation of teaching is associated with collegial decision-making processes including tenure, promotion and salary review, right of first refusal and for review of academic programs.... Most universities advocate that peer evaluations form an essential part of the evidence to assess a candidate's teaching effectiveness....

Summative peer evaluation can include formative aspects although the primary purpose shall be to provide evidence for career decision points. The formative aspects of peer evaluation can include the meeting between the teacher and reviewer to discuss the evaluation process. Another formative portion of peer evaluation is the written assessment following the completion of the review that should be shared with the teacher. Alternatively, we recommend that the department head or dean meet with the candidate to advise them of the outcome and share suggestions on ways to improve teaching. In most evaluation processes, the sharing of outcomes with participants completes the feedback loop and forms an important part of the learning process for all concerned.

Assessment of teaching performance should be based on a series of evaluations of a candidate's teaching performance and teaching materials over a period of time. The peer evaluation will consider all aspects of teaching and evidence of performance. Peer evaluations should be obtained on an ongoing basis.

Role of Evaluation Reviewers

For the purpose of peer evaluation, the peer reviewers should be based in the same department or non-departmentalized college, wherever possible, as the teacher being evaluated. Peer reviewers need not be content experts. It is recommended that reviewers be tenured department or college members or associate members whose rank is equivalent to or higher than the candidate's. (Reviewers with potential biases should be avoided.) The teacher being reviewed should also identify potential conflicts of interest. Reasonableness and common sense should prevail in such matters.

Departments, colleges or relevant teaching committees should adapt guidelines relevant to their disciplines and the circumstances of their department or college. Department or college guidelines should be provided to reviewers to ensure that they understand their roles and responsibilities. Training of peer reviewers is important especially for first-time reviewers to ensure that the review process is understood, best practices are known and that fair and objective evaluations are produced. From time to time and upon request from colleges, the Gwenna Moss Teaching and Learning Centre will offer workshops on the peer evaluation of teaching. Peer review of teaching should be an integral part of the teaching activities of the departments and colleges.

The University appreciates the time commitment required to conduct a proper peer evaluation of teaching. For example, it may take one or two hours to review the course materials and examinations, to observe classroom teaching, a couple of hours to prepare a written report and time to meet and discuss the reviewer's findings with the instructor.   Evaluators are encouraged to list their work as part of their contribution to teaching activities on their respective c.v.'s and should be a part of the work listed in the update of their annual activities report. As with proper peer review of research activities, proper peer review of teaching is important to assess the activities of teachers and it should be valued accordingly. Departments and colleges are advised to recognize the contributions of peer evaluators when assigning duties and when rewarding meritorious performance.

Frequency

It is important that evaluations be conducted serially so as to provide a reasonable sampling of evidence over a time period. It is recommended that one course per year be evaluated by a peer for each teacher in a probationary appointment. As a minimum, there should be no fewer than four peer evaluations for over a six-year probationary period. Departments and colleges should determine the frequency of evaluations for those who have achieved tenure, permanent or continuing status and those who have been promoted to the highest faculty rank at the University but it is recommended that such evaluations occur every three years after achieving tenure or promotion to full professor. Peer evaluations within the final three years of appointment preceding retirement will be conducted at the request of the teacher. While the frequency of peer evaluations may seem onerous, it is important to provide good information for teachers so they can improve as teachers by making them accountable for their teaching performance and methods.

The timing of the peer review is also important. Peer reviews should not be conducted in the first two weeks or last two weeks of a course offering.

If these practices cannot be adopted, a written explanation of the reasons for not conducting multiple observations and multi-level assessments shall be provided for the record.

Sessional lecturers will not be subject to peer evaluations except as required by the formal teaching assessments set out in their Collective Agreement.

Criteria for Peer Evaluation

Before the peer review is conducted, the reviewer and the reviewee should discuss the process and understand their respective roles in the review in accordance with the relevant standards and institutional, college and departmental policies.

For best practice, it is recommended that information on the candidate's teaching be gathered from two different people before a major decision is made. It is suggested that each reviewer should observe classroom performance on two different occasions for each evaluation. Over time, it is also preferred if information is gathered on teaching at various course levels.

The appendices provide guidance about the dimensions and factors that might be considered for a peer review of teaching. Academic units should review the *University Standards for Promotion and Tenure* on teaching ability and performance and in particular Table II—Evaluation of Teaching. The Table identifies teaching roles, aspects to be assessed and items and activities to be reviewed. Peer evaluation should embrace the various aspects of teaching including the criteria listed below. All peer evaluations will culminate in a written assessment. As a minimum, criteria to be evaluated should include:

1. review of classroom performance
2. quality of examinations
3. course outlines and course materials
4. syllabi
5. reading materials
6. reading lists
7. laboratory manuals
8. workbooks
9. classroom assignments.

Sample questions and processes on the criteria are provided in the appendices. Conclusions should be based on evidence from documentation that has been provided and knowledge supported by a review of materials and classroom performance. The review should be comprehensive and comparative and focus on overall performance.... A best practice is to ensure that the outcomes of the peer evaluation are shared with the teacher. This can be done in writing by the reviewer or by discussions with the reviewer or the department head or dean. Information gathered from peer evaluations (and evaluations from students) may form part of the information used by a department head or dean when advising candidates on their career progress. The advice can be formative and provide guidance on what is required to improve teaching effectiveness.

Departments and colleges that currently have peer evaluation processes or instruments are encouraged to review them to ensure they incorporate best practices and meet standard criteria for peer evaluation of teaching. Four examples of instruments used for peer evaluation are appended. Departments and colleges that do not currently have instruments in place to guide evaluators are asked to consider adopting one of these instruments or to develop their own to meet their needs. The weight given to such evaluations should also be discussed by the academic unit and consideration given to the variety of information gathered on teaching (peer, student and self-evaluation). Departments and colleges should also consider the weight given to peer evaluations early in the career of a teacher as compared to those given closer to career decision points and later in their careers; teachers must be given the opportunity to improve their teaching over the course of their academic career and should be encouraged to be innovative and effective in the classroom.

[Author's note: A list of resources is included in the original statement.]

Next Steps

This Framework does not address peer review of clinical teaching, courses in performing and studio arts or those taught by teams. There are gaps in these areas at other institutions. It is intended that the appropriate academic units will develop peer review processes in these areas. To the extent possible, modified peer review processes should be consistent with this Framework and the Principles of the Evaluation of Teaching at the University of Saskatchewan.

University of Saskatchewan. (1998). *A framework for planning at the University of Saskatchewan: Best practices.* Saskatoon, Saskatchewan: Author.

University of Saskatchewan. (2002). *Peer consultation programme.* Saskatoon, Saskatchewan: Author.

University of Saskatchewan. (2002). *Principles of evaluation of teaching at the University of Saskatchewan.* Saskatoon, Saskatchewan: Author.

University of Saskatchewan. (2002). *University of Saskatchewan standards for promotion and tenure.* Saskatoon, Saskatchewan: Author.

Reprinted with permission.

Chapter 3

Major Design Elements of a Peer Review of Teaching System

This chapter will provide an overview of the components of a peer review of teaching system, focusing primarily on the following elements:

- Statement of teaching values and purpose of peer review activities
- Identification of which faculty members will be involved
- Logistics of the review: when and how they will occur
- Criteria: areas of teaching that will be reviewed and desired characteristics
- Evidence to be collected for peer review
- Standards to be used in judgment
- Instruments available to reviewers for performing the reviews
- Procedures for conducting and recording the reviews
- Provisions for preparation of reviewers
- Provisions for revision of the plan

Plans may be developed at various levels of campus organization, from the central administrative level to the department or program level. They may be developed for faculty in various appointments, such as part-time lecturers, full-time faculty, or graduate teaching assistants. They may be designed for specific functions, such as post-tenure review or a teaching award, but most frequently they will be developed as part of the annual review and advancement cycle for tenure-track faculty. The complexity of a plan will depend on its purpose and reach. In the discussion that follows, a broad application is assumed; for more specific purposes, such as making teaching award judgments, adaptation will be necessary.

Statement of Teaching Values and Purpose of Peer Review Activities

An important opening to any written plan for peer review of teaching should contain an expression of the originating unit's values on teaching. While a general affirmation of the value of teaching to the unit is a starting point, it is more helpful that the statement be situated in the particular context. For example, it might refer to the urban context of the institution, the importance of the preparation of engineering professionals to modern society, or the like. If the institution or unit has in the past espoused principles of teaching and learning, standards for effective teaching, or any related values, they should be included. Other statements aligning the peer review plans with major institutional values are important in this opening section. If supporting references to the scholarly literature on peer evaluation are deemed helpful, these should be added as well.

A clear description of the plan's purpose should follow. Is the plan to provide for peer review for a very specific purpose, such as judging candidates for new faculty positions or determining the renewal of part-time lecturers, or is it to be the basis for many kinds of faculty advancement activities? A very important distinction in this regard is whether the peer review activities are intended for formative or summative purposes, or both. Will information generated by peer reviewers be used solely for improvement purposes and belong to the faculty members who are reviewed, or will it be part of the permanent record and be used to make judgments about merit increases, promotion, tenure, hiring, or awards? These are important clarifications to make.

Identifying the Faculty Members Involved

The plan will need to identify those faculty members to be reviewed and those who will serve as reviewers. It should address whether the plan is for post-tenure review or for graduate teaching assistants, or for all teaching faculty. If a particular group is specified for peer review, it is desirable to state why peer review will be especially helpful for this group.

Identifying which faculty will serve as reviewers is another key element of the plan. Statements should specify whether peers within or outside the institution, or both, will be doing the reviews. The type of faculty appointment that the reviewer should have, disciplinary background, level of experience, and other factors that have been determined to be important need to be included in the plan at this point.

There are no rigid guidelines for making these decisions, which are very context-dependent. Normally, peer reviewers are expected to have senior status to the person being reviewed, yet in some forms of reciprocal peer review for formative purposes, colleagues at the same level do the reviews. Traditionally, peer reviewers for promotion and tenure purposes are colleagues at an advanced rank from another institution, yet it is often difficult for these colleagues to comment on teaching performance unless appropriate materials are sent to them. In cases of distance education, the use of external peers is easier since they can experience the courses of the person under review more closely by accessing them electronically.

The expertise and background of the reviewer are often involved in selection and are important for the trustworthiness of the process. It is common practice to distinguish between peers who are qualified to comment on subject matter expertise and those who can take a more general look at teaching performance. Although as Cosser (1998) points out, there is divided opinion on how important it is to match the scholarly expertise of the peer reviewer with that of the person being reviewed, in general the advice supports the use of a panel of reviewers over time. That is, different reviewers with varied backgrounds can review the same person so that the multiple reviews together can reflect different perspectives.

Hutchings (1996b) speaks to this issue, saying that

> the "community of judgment" for teaching is actually several different communities. Some aspects of teaching, like classroom performance, are probably best reviewed by peers within the institution; others, including syllabi and other materials might benefit from external peer review by experts at the national level. (p. 228)

Because academic work can be so specialized, it is often difficult to locate subject matter peers within an institution. In interdisciplinary teaching situations, a team of experts may be needed. While many faculty can make a determination of content quality when judging an introductory course in their unit, they are much less likely to be able to make such judgments in advanced seminars, which often treat specific topic areas in which they have not done major scholarly work. For content quality decisions, then, an outside expert is often needed, and although sharing materials electronically now makes the teaching of a particular faculty member more available for external review, it is still a complicated enough process to warrant limited use. Occasional certifications of content accuracy may be more feasible than regular attention to this area when the faculty member under review teaches in specialized areas.

Taylor and Richardson (2001) point out that for electronic materials, such as web-based courses, a third community of judgment is needed in addition to subject matter and content experts: educational designers with expertise in instructional technology, who can comment on navigation, use of the medium, and other issues that might not be within the expertise of many faculty peers.

Distinguishing between a peer reviewer for formative purposes, who will be a mentor and coach, and a peer reviewer for summative purposes, who will advise on personnel decisions, is often recommended, based on the belief that faculty members under review will feel freer to discuss problems and confide in peers playing the coach role if they know that these people will not be involved in making personnel decisions down the line. However, given the size of most academic units and the disciplinary subspecialties within them, it is often impractical to designate separate individuals for these functions. Plans should be based on the realities of the context rather than the ideal situation.

In his study of the review of teaching portfolios for summative purposes, Centra (2000) found that the ratings of peers selected by the faculty member being reviewed did not correlate well with student ratings or the ratings of the administrator and a peer chosen independently. This finding might underscore that for formative purposes, individuals being reviewed might indicate a preference for a particular reviewer, but for summative purposes, it is best to have others select the reviewers.

Logistics of the Review: When and How Often

Peer review plans for specific purposes, such as making hiring decisions or judging awards, are obviously attached to specified times. For more comprehensive reviews, however, it is important to determine when peer reviews should occur for both formative and summative purposes. Should tenure-track faculty be reviewed for summative purposes by peers every year, or only at key points, such as the third year and the sixth year? Should they receive formative peer review continuously through a mentoring system? Should post-tenure faculty be reviewed every year or only when a specific series of occurrences or results of annual review specify that a review should take place (triggered review)?

Given that reliability increases with repeated reviews and that continuous peer review can initiate dialogue and transform the culture of an academic unit into one where exchange about teaching is part of the everyday discourse, it is desirable to encourage frequent peer review. The practicalities of time and availability of reviewers dictate, however, that plans might set more modest expectations. It is also a good idea to distinguish between full reviews and partial reviews. For example, a plan might indicate that at least two classroom observations per year will be required for pre-tenure faculty (amounting to twelve by the time they are preparing their dossiers), but that preparation and review of a teaching portfolio will occur only at the third and sixth years.

At the heart of every peer review of teaching system are three essential building blocks: criteria, evidence, and standards. Although other components, such as procedures for choosing a peer, timing of the reviews, and reconsideration policies, are also important, a good system of peer review is characterized by its ability to articulate what the unit values in teaching, where good teaching will be manifest to a reviewer, and how the reviewer should determine levels of performance.

Criteria

According to Centra (1993), criteria "define what aspects of a performance will be evaluated" (p. 6). In Angelo's (1996) definition, "criteria of exemplary teaching will tell us what to look for" (p. 58). Although these statements seem straightforward, it is quite challenging for most people to name what it is that they think are the essential elements of good teaching. Johnson and Ryan (2000) state, "One of the most fundamental challenges facing the evaluation of college teaching is defining specific expectations of faculty in regard to teaching" (p. 110). As discussed earlier, there are several reasons why defining criteria is challenging, some rooted in traditional beliefs that "there is nothing to teaching but telling" or "teaching only involves knowledge of content" or "good teaching cannot be analyzed—you just know it when you see it." Other reasons have to do with the situation-specific nature of teaching, which takes on a variety of forms; the complexity of the teaching act; and the value-laden nature of definitions of good teaching. A look at the literature on teaching effectiveness reveals a complex and often contradictory record of claims (Chism, 2004). All in all, identifying criteria is difficult.

One way to approach the task of identifying criteria is to break down criteria into categories and characteristics. For example, categories might include advising, lecturing, or designing courses, all of which are aspects of teaching that might constitute the focus of peer review of teaching. Characteristics associated with these categories might include currency of subject expertise, clarity, or interpersonal rapport—positive qualities associated with effectiveness within these categories.

CATEGORIES FROM TEACHING TASK TAXONOMIES

There are several sources that provide help in thinking about categories of teaching. In a book suggesting that we might think of the different tasks of teaching being performed by teams rather than individuals, Donald (2000, pp. 44–45) lists the following categories of teaching responsibilities:

Provision of Intellectual Context:
- Explaining educational goals
- Understanding the institutional context
- Understanding students
- Providing the disciplinary context
- Providing a learning community
- Establishing student responsibility for learning

Instructional Planning and Evaluation:
- Designing
- Representing knowledge
- Selecting teaching strategies
- Adapting to student characteristics
- Aligning instruction
- Aligning through monitoring and evaluating

The chapters in *Teaching Alone, Teaching Together* by Bess and Associates (2000) go into finer detail about the specific tasks involved in each kind of teaching. For example, the list for an effective discussion group leader contains the following subtasks (Tiberius & Tipping, 2000, p. 111):

Encourage and Maintain Discussion.
- Encourage a climate of acceptance to promote freedom of expression.
- Choose topics that provide stimulus for discussion.
- Choose a topic of interest to the group and define it clearly.
- Create an informal atmosphere.
- After getting the group going, serve primarily as a guide.

Keep the Discussion on Topic.
- Summarize when appropriate.
- Clarify the topic.
- Clarify the goals.

Promote Sharing among Learners
- Set ground rules.
- Encourage members to listen to one another and hear the viewpoints of others.
- Encourage balanced interaction among the learners.

Encourage Participation and Involvement.
- Listen to students actively.
- Provide opportunities for practice or rehearsal.
- Provide opportunities for self-expression.

Encourage Awareness of Group Process.
- Role model good group process.
- Point out process issues to the group.

Deal with Group Difficulties.
- Deal with disruptive students.
- Reduce destructive conflict and competition.
- Help students who lack motivation.
- Deal with uncooperative students.

While basing a peer review of teaching system on such a fine-grained analysis of every teaching task would make it unduly cumbersome, contemplation of the various components that constitute teaching is a good exercise in the development of a system. Grouping tasks into categories or prioritizing tasks into categories of major focus will help developers of a system to tailor it to the teaching components of importance within the context. The specific tasks can later be the basis for instruments that will be completed by the reviewer.

Additional insights into the possible criteria that might be the basis for peer review of teaching come from the Meta-Profession project of the Center for Educational Design and Assessment (n.d.). This project distinguishes between "base skills" and "meta-profession skills" in faculty life:

> A college professor must perform at a professional level a variety of roles that require expertise and skills in areas that often extend beyond the faculty member's specific area of scholarly expertise or "Base Profession." Thus, the skill sets required by faculty to perform in these roles are divided into two general categories: Base Profession Skills and the *additional* Meta-Profession Skills.

Within the teaching dimension of faculty work, the project organizes the base profession skills into content expertise, practice or clinical skills, and research techniques—all competencies that instructors in a given discipline must have before one observes teaching actions or skills. The project lists 19 meta-profession skills for teaching, ranging from instructional design, instructional delivery, and assessment skills—ones that are often associated with teaching—to technical writing, graphic design, and personnel management skills—ones that are certainly involved in most teaching roles, but less often explicitly identified as categories of skills that teachers must have. The Meta-Profession project further distinguishes across the settings in which these skills are used, such as standard classroom, tutorial, and clinic/practicum.

Others such as Elton (1996), Hativa and Goodyear (2002), and Pratt (1997) speak to teacher beliefs and assumptions as critical to evaluating the work that is done. Exploring the basis for teaching is fundamental to formative evaluation and in summative evaluation can be demonstrated through portfolio reflections and philosophy of teaching statements.

The work on identifying categories of faculty work and associated skills helps create awareness that any review of teaching focused exclusively on classroom performance is limited. It also helps those developing systems of peer review to begin listing categories appropriate for review.

Desired Qualities of Teaching Effectiveness

When associating qualities of desired performance to the categories, issues of values and traditions come to the fore. The literature on teaching effectiveness might be explored as a way to identify dispassionate, "scientifically-derived" characteristics, but it is a complex literature and difficult to access. Murray (1995) provides an overview, summarizing the literature by saying that excellent teachers care about their learners and learning, believe that their students can learn and communicate this expectation, and stress collaboration. One recent summary (Chism, 2004) contains parallel findings from a representative study in each of six methodological schools of study regarding teaching effectiveness. The limited conclusions that Chism draws from this exercise single out such characteristics as enthusiasm, clarity, organization, and rapport as related to teaching effectiveness in presentation settings. Less information was available about other learning settings, such as active learning environments.

Some scholars distinguish between characteristics that can be labeled with low inference and high inference terms. Low inference terms are those that minimize the judgments reviewers would have to make about behaviors, while high inference terms involve more judgment. An example of a low inference term to describe a behavior would be "knows students' names," a behavior that would be fairly easy to identify consistently. A higher inference term is "friendly," which varies in how it is displayed and judged according to the personality of the teacher and the perceptions of the reviewer. Generally, it is thought that low inference terms help to make judgments more consistent, but they can fail to capture a holistic sense of what is being judged, so generally both kinds of terms are needed in the review of teaching.

CLASSIC LISTS OF CRITERIA

In the three classic lists of criteria for peer review systems that follow, categories and characteristics are interspersed. They are listed here to illustrate selectivity and prioritization. Of all the areas of teaching that might be selected, these scholars recommended only certain areas.

Seldin (1984, pp. 139–140) includes the following:

1. Selection and mastery of course content
2. Appropriateness of course objectives and instructional materials
3. Appropriate methodology for teaching specified sections of courses
4. Appropriate techniques to foster and measure student learning
5. Course organization
6. Student achievement based on exams, projects, presentations, and reports
7. Concern for and interest in teaching
8. Homework assignments, textbooks, and handouts

Cohen and McKeachie (1980, pp. 151–152) enumerate four broad areas for colleague assessment, including the second-order function of looking at evidence from other peers. The areas are elements of course design, instructional methods and materials, evaluation of students, and integration and interpretation of information gathered by others. Specific subtopics are included under each area:

1. Course goals/course content
   - Appropriateness of course goals
   - Coverage of basic course content
   - Currency of course content
   - Appropriateness of student work requirements
2. Instructional methods and materials
   - Suitability of methods of instruction to course goals
   - Appropriateness of reading list for the course
   - Reasonableness of time and efforts required to complete assignments

- Appropriateness of handouts and learning aids
- Suitability of media materials to course
3. Evaluation of students' work
   - Inclusion of higher order cognitive processes on exams and assignments
   - Reasonableness of length and difficulty of examinations
   - Degree of cognitive challenge of written assignments
   - Reasonableness of length and effort required to complete writing assignments
   - Appropriateness of grading criteria
4. Integration and interpretation
   - Interpretation of student ratings within the context of the course that is rated
   - Determination of criteria used for evaluation
   - Weighting of criteria used in determining teaching effectiveness

French-Lazovik's (1981, pp. 79–81) treatment of the issue of areas that peers should assess advocates asking the following questions:

1. What is the quality of materials used in teaching?
   - Are these materials current?
   - Do they represent the best work in the field?
   - Are they adequate and appropriate to course goals?
   - Do they represent superficial or thorough coverage of course materials?
2. What kind of intellectual tasks were set by the teacher for the students (or did the teacher succeed in getting students to set for themselves), and how did the students perform?
   - What was the level of intellectual performance achieved by the students?
   - What kinds of work was given an A? a B? a C?
   - Did the students learn what the department curriculum expected for this course?
   - How adequately do the tests or assignments represent the kinds of student performance specified in the course objectives?
3. How knowledgeable is this faculty member in the subjects taught?
   - Has the instructor kept in thoughtful contact with developments in his or her field?
   - Is there evidence of acquaintance with the ideas and findings of other scholars?
4. Has this faculty member assumed responsibilities related to the department's or university's teaching mission?
   - Has he or she become a departmental or college citizen in regard to teaching responsibilities?

- Does this faculty member recognize problems that hinder good teaching, and does he or she take a responsible part in trying to solve them?
- Is the involvement of the faculty member appropriate to his or her academic level?

5. To what extent is this faculty member trying to achieve excellence in teaching?
   - Has he or she sought feedback about teaching quality, explored alternative teaching methods, made changes to increase student learning?
   - Has he or she sought aid in trying new teaching ideas?
   - Has he or she developed special teaching materials or participated in cooperative efforts aimed at upgrading teaching quality?

Table 3.1 presents a summary chart with possibilities for both categories and characteristics. This can be used as a worksheet to decide which are appropriate and which are not, as well as to add categories and characteristics that are not on the list but are specific to the context of the review.

Finally, attention to the weighting of criteria is also important. For example, is it more important to the academic unit that classes are well designed or that teachers engage in research on teaching? How much emphasis should be put on each in evaluating overall performance? Should these weights be different for different faculty members? For example, in a system developed for Texas A&M University, Pritchard, Watson, Kelly, and Paquin (1998) reported the following weights: effectiveness of classroom teaching (58%), effective interpersonal skills related to teaching (13%), efforts to improve teaching (12%), influential scholarship of teaching (10%), and student advising (7%). Not many systems will attempt this precision, but discussion of priorities among clusters of activities is needed during the development of a system. A further consideration is the applicability of these weightings: Should they be different for different faculty members? For example, if one faculty member is particularly good at advising doctoral students, should the weighting of that activity for him or her be greater than for others who are devoting more time to undergraduate instruction?

Evidence

Once a list of criteria has been developed, it is important to think through where a reviewer might find evidence of performance for each criterion. For example, if a given criterion calls for frequent and helpful feedback to students, there are a variety of ways to determine whether this criterion is being met. A reviewer might look at the syllabus to learn how many times there is official feedback (tests and other assignments that will be graded or receive response); the reviewer might look at samples of comments on student

Table 3.1 Possible Categories and Characteristics to be Assessed in Peer Review of Teaching Systems

Category	Characteristics
Content Knowledge	<ul><li>Mastery/accuracy</li><li>Appropriate selection</li><li>Currency</li><li>Breadth—knowledgeable of other fields and perspectives</li><li>Tolerance of diverse points of view</li></ul>
Course Design	<ul><li>Appropriate challenge</li><li>Clarity of goals and objectives</li><li>Alignment with unit curriculum</li><li>Inclusive of motivational considerations</li></ul>
Teaching Methods	<ul><li>Worthwhile activities</li><li>Variety of approaches</li><li>Clarity and organization</li><li>Effective speaking skills</li><li>Effective student interaction skills</li><li>Accommodating of disabilities</li></ul>
Student Communication	<ul><li>Accessibility to students</li><li>Clarity</li><li>Responsiveness</li></ul>
Assessment	<ul><li>Appropriate design of tests, performance tasks</li><li>Alignment of assessment and goals</li><li>High level of cognitive challenge</li><li>Clear, appropriate grading criteria</li><li>High overall standards</li></ul>
Materials	<ul><li>Suitability</li><li>Appropriateness</li><li>Currency</li><li>Alignment with course goals</li><li>Thoroughness, depth</li><li>Creativity</li><li>Editing</li></ul>
Use of Technology	<ul><li>Appropriate use of medium</li><li>Technological functionality</li><li>Interactivity</li><li>Attractiveness of design</li><li>Alignment with course goals</li></ul>
Student Learning Results	<ul><li>Performance</li><li>Impact</li><li>Engagement</li></ul>

continued on next page

Table 3.1 *continued*

Category	Characteristics
Leadership in Department/School/Nation	▪ Quality of contribution ▪ Quantity of contribution
Scholarship of Teaching and Learning	▪ Based on important problems or issues ▪ Appropriateness of research methods ▪ Quality of data collection and analysis ▪ Clarity of presentation of findings ▪ Peer review
Teaching Development	▪ Reflective practice ▪ Extent of participation in activities ▪ Innovation
Mentoring, Advising	▪ Accessibility to students ▪ Quality of advice ▪ Knowledge of options and resources for students ▪ Interpersonal skills
Special Contexts (field-based teaching, service-learning, team teaching)	▪ Modeling of rapport with patients/clients ▪ Quality of relationship with onsite preceptor/supervisor ▪ Collaboration with co-teacher

papers, email, or other feedback that the instructor provides; the reviewer observing class sessions might note the incidence of feedback during the class and the perceived helpfulness of it. Student reviews of the faculty member, either on course evaluation items asking about feedback, or through letters collected at the time of promotion and/or tenure decisions, can also attest to the helpfulness and frequency of feedback.

Often, some of the evidence for peer review use does not originate with the peer reviewer. There is a second-order function of peer review: Peers are asked to review judgments and evidence submitted by others. For example, in a promotion consideration, peers will evaluate a dossier containing multiple kinds of evidence from various sources, ranging from student ratings of instruction to self-assessment by the person being reviewed to colleagues' opinions of course syllabi. The peer can thus be involved at two stages: providing an initial commentary on some aspect of the teaching for either formative or summative purposes (contributing evidence), or judging the accumulated evidence from others, or both.

Multiple types of evidence are available for making judgments on teaching performance questions; the reviewer is not limited to records of classroom observation. In enumerating the kinds of evidence that can be explored during period reviews, French-Lazovik (1981, pp. 76–78) reveals the wide range of evidence that can be surveyed:

1. Course outlines
2. Syllabi
3. Reading lists
4. Texts, study guides, non-print materials, and handouts
5. Problem sets, assignments
6. Copies of graded examinations, examples of graded research papers
7. Examples of teacher's feedback to students on written work
8. Grade distribution and descriptions of student performances
9. Examples of completed assignments
10. Records of service on department or institutional committees dealing with teaching issues (curriculum, honors program, etc.)
11. Descriptions of activities in supervising graduate students learning to teach
12. Evidence of the design of new courses
13. Statements of what activities the faculty member has engaged in to improve his or her teaching
14. Examples of questionnaires used for formative purposes
15. Examples of changes made on the basis of feedback.

To these, Malik (1996) adds the reflective memo composed by the faculty member being reviewed. Bernstein, Burnett, Goodburn, and Savory (2006) and Quinlan (1996) discuss the course portfolio as a way to present many of these documents coherently (see Chapter 9).

Individual departments will choose to focus on some of these areas and types of evidence or on additional ones that they identify. Different areas for review or types of evidence may also be identified at the college or institutional levels.

Table 3.2, an excerpt from a document developed for faculty preparing dossiers for promotion and tenure at Indiana University–Purdue University Indianapolis (IUPUI) shows how the criteria categories (arrayed down the left column) have been matched with the sources of evidence according to the structural components of the dossier (along the top row). This excerpt is for the teaching component of the dossier and gives specific suggestions for how evidence for each category can be supplied by the person preparing the dossier. It also gives reviewers a map to use in locating potential evidence for making judgments.

Table 3.3 provides a generic chart suggesting sources of evidence for the criteria selected.

Table 3.2 Documentation of Teaching Performance in IUPUI Faculty Dossiers *(reprinted with permission)*

Dimensions of Teaching Performance	Section II: Personal Statement	Potential Locations		
		Section III: Narrative Contained in Evaluation of Teaching	CV (part of Section I)	Peer Review (external and internal—may be part of Sections I or III)
Teaching load		Details on students mentored, advised, etc.	List of courses, etc.	Comment on relative size of load
Teaching goals	List of goals		List of formal activities	Comment on fit with IUPUI and unit goals
Continuing professional development	Description of activities undertaken	Details of workshops attended, study, reading, etc.	List of formal activities	
Use of exemplary teaching methods	Description of methods	Details on specific methods such as teaching with technology, use of problem-based learning, service-learning, or other innovative methods, inclusive teaching		Local peer review, external if knowledgeable
Quality of teaching	Reflective comments	Student rating summaries, peer review of class performance or materials		Local peer review, external if knowledgeable
Evidence of student learning	Reflective comments	Results of nationally normed tests, pre/post evaluations of course knowledge gains, analysis of student work, student/alumni reports, approach toward PULs (for UG courses)		Local peer review, external if knowledgeable
Ethics	Self-report	Student report		Local peer review
Scholarship of teaching and national leadership	Descriptions of scholarly approach	Details, commentary on activities listed in CV	Publications, presentations, national leadership on teaching in discipline	Local or external peer review
Course and curriculum development	Self-report	Details on CV entries	List of commit-tees, etc.	Local peer review, external if knowledgeable
Recognition (grants, awards)		Details on CV entries, if needed	List of recognitions	

Table 3.3 Possible Sources of Evidence for Assessing Selected Categories of Teaching Performance in Peer Review of Teaching Systems

Category	Possible Source of Peer Review Evidence
Content Knowledge	▪ Examination of syllabus ▪ Examination of course materials and tests ▪ Classroom observation records ▪ Scholarly record
Course Design	▪ Examination of syllabus and materials ▪ Philosophy of teaching statement
Teaching Methods	▪ Classroom observation records ▪ Examination of course materials ▪ Examination of student ratings scores ▪ Record of teaching awards or honors
Student Communication	▪ Examination of student ratings scores ▪ Classroom observation records ▪ Samples of emails, letters
Assessment	▪ Examination of tests or performance tasks ▪ Samples of comments on graded work ▪ Student ratings scores on assessment items
Materials	▪ Examination of materials
Use of Technology	▪ Examination of electronic components ▪ Student ratings scores on these components
Student Learning Results	▪ Examination of graded work or products ▪ Comparisons on normed scales, if available ▪ Reports of instructors in related areas ▪ Student ratings scores on related items
Leadership in Department/School/Nation	▪ CV documentation ▪ Awards or testimony of colleagues
Scholarship of Teaching and Learning	▪ CV documentation ▪ Print products ▪ Honors or awards for this work
Teaching Development	▪ Philosophy of teaching statement ▪ Other reflective documents ▪ CV record of participation in development activities
Mentoring, Advising	▪ Documentation of advising record ▪ Sample of communications with students ▪ Student ratings scores on related items ▪ Records of advisee achievements
Special Contexts (field-based teaching, service-learning, team teaching)	▪ Sample of communications with colleagues ▪ Site observation records ▪ Examination of materials

Standards

Although it is difficult to identify clear criteria and to associate them with locations for evidence, the enumeration of standards is perhaps the most challenging aspect of framing a peer review process. Standards are the guide to the expected quality of specific aspects of teaching. They help the reviewer to determine whether a given performance is poor, fair, good, excellent, or something in between. They are saturated with the values of the context. Although many would prefer not to articulate standards, feeling that this action removes discretion and is essentially reductionist in nature, the fact remains that standards are being applied every time a judgment is made. Whether these are personal or shared, consistent or inconsistent depends on the extent to which they are articulated. It is understood that these standards must be generated and interpreted locally in the department or school, as well as at the campus level.

How specific should standards be? Is it reasonable, for example, to state that a faculty member who generates more than one peer-reviewed product of the scholarship of teaching and learning is "excellent," one who generates one product is "acceptable," and one who generates no products in a given year is "unacceptable"? Or, is it better to state that a faculty member whose record shows "thoughtful, original work and productivity superior to that of colleagues" on this dimension would be rated "excellent"?

Elton (1996) distinguishes between "competence" and "excellence" by drawing attention to the thoughtfulness and spirit of innovation behind teaching practice:

> The first criterion for excellence is to be highly competent . . . but it is only one criterion, because excellent teachers are far more than that. To start with they are reflective practitioners, that is they seriously reflect on what they are doing and why they are doing it, draw conclusions from that, and thereby improve what they are doing in a systematic manner. An innovative teacher looks where perhaps accepted practice either never was adequate or is no longer adequate in a changing system. (p. 34)

He goes on to state that engaging in certain activities, such as leading a course team, doing the scholarship of teaching, and the like, are all markers of excellence.

Determining standards is similar to creating rubrics for grading student work. The characteristics of quality and quantity entailed in assigning grades for performance are articulated in such a grid. Listing these requires clarifying expectations. While this can be an arduous and tedious process, the benefits are the same as for grading rubrics: The process helps the person presenting the work to identify goals and it helps the reviewer to be consistent in making judgments. A sample table of standards for some categories of teaching is included in Table 3.4. When developing such a table for peer review within an institution or academic unit, it is important to be as specific as possible without being arbitrary or overly prescriptive. Although quantitative measures (e.g., at least five major points of feedback occurred in each course) may help the reviewer to assign a rating, they often do not take context or quality into account. It is also important not to mix logical categories across a ratings continuum, such as designating a measure of quality for an excellent rating and a measure of quantity for an unsatisfactory rating on the same item.

Table 3.4 Sample Standards for Selected Categories in Peer Review of Teaching Systems (examples rather than complete statement)

Category	Excellent	Satisfactory	Unacceptable
Content Knowledge	• Cutting edge • Deep grasp • Broad • Actively exploring multiple perspectives	• Current • Accurate • Discipline-based • Accommodating of multiple perspectives	• Outdated • Inaccurate • Narrow • Intolerant of multiple perspectives
Course Design	• Extensive description of goals and objectives • Explicitly aligned with overall curriculum • High expectations with plan for student success	• Clear goals and objectives stated • Aligned with overall curriculum • Appropriate level of challenge	• No/unclear goals and objectives • Not aligned with overall curriculum • Inappropriate level of challenge or challenge for students
Assessment	• Creative, relevant tests and tasks • Extensive feedback • Frequent points of assessment	• Well-designed tests or tasks • Specific feedback • Regular assessment	• Poorly designed tests, tasks • Little or vague feedback • Infrequent assessment
Leadership in Department/School/Nation	• Extensive participation • Excellent record of effectiveness	• Satisfactory record of effectiveness • Routine contributions	• Record of ineffectiveness • Little or no participation
Scholarship of Teaching and Learning	• Extensive publications and presentations • Recognized excellence by external peers	• Some record of shared scholarly work on teaching • Recognition internally	• Little or no scholarly work on teaching • No reputation for excellence

Instruments for Performing Reviews

Any discussion of criteria and standards will be operationalized by forms, checklists, or other instruments that will help the reviewer to focus on those areas of teaching that have been specified and apply agreed-upon standards in making judgments or in informing coaching activities. Depending on the purpose and scope of the plan, there may be only one form or many. For peer review applications to teaching awards, for example, a form that calls for a reviewer to rate a portfolio on specific dimensions might be the only instrument needed. For a more encompassing plan, forms to be used for classroom observation, syllabus review, review of course handouts, and the like may be developed. Part II of this volume provides starting points for the construction of these forms. In addition, Richlin (2006) provides a rich resource of rubrics for assessing many common kinds of instructional documents. Many options are available.

Procedures for Conducting and Recording the Reviews

For each type of peer review activity that the plan specifies, it is important to outline how the activity will take place. For example, if classroom observation is a part of the plan, will the observations take place unannounced or at the prior agreement of reviewer and person being reviewed? Will the presence of the observer be announced to the class members or not? Where will the observer sit? Will the observer take part in the class or not? Should the observer talk with students before or after class or not? Will the observation be preceded by a discussion of the context and a sharing of course syllabus and other materials? Will it be followed by a post-observation debriefing?

Similarly, for materials or portfolio review, which materials will be a part of the review? Will the instructor submit a written or oral commentary on the materials? Will the review be preceded or followed by discussion between peer reviewer and person being reviewed?

Plans should indicate how the peer reviewers will record their judgments. In the case of formative review, much of the exchange might be oral and informal. For summative purposes, a standard format that becomes part of the personnel record is usually required. The time frame for submission of reports of peer review activities should be stated in the plan. The length of time that records will be kept in the personnel folder should also be specified.

Part II of this volume presents ideas for procedures on common methods of peer review.

Provisions for Preparation of Reviewers

An often overlooked part of the peer review plan is how peer reviewers will be prepared. It is frequently assumed that peers are ready to do reviews and confident about their ability to do so, but experience suggests that this is not usually the case. If faculty members are involved in the development of a plan, they have already had the advantage of working through the decisions involved, which is a form of preparation since they understand the rationale for the plan. If a plan has been developed by others, however, it will be necessary for faculty reviewers to receive orientation to the system.

A good way to help new reviewers (and those to be reviewed) understand the system is to conduct mock reviews using videotapes with classroom observation instruments and sample materials for materials review instruments. Engaging faculty members in using the forms on a trial basis helps to calibrate reviews: The discussion and comparisons that occur as faculty do the mock reviews make them aware of the need to be consistent and use the standards that have been articulated. If the institution has an administrative support unit dealing with teaching and learning, the staff from this unit might help in the preparation of reviewers.

Provisions for Revision of the Plan

Every plan should be viewed as a work in progress. Although it is important that there be some continuity of approach over time, peer review of teaching plans must be adjusted to changing circumstances and modified when flaws become apparent. The temptation to view the development of a plan as completed should yield to the recognition that a plan must be reviewed carefully after an initial implementation period, and then regularly as it is subsequently used. The advice of faculty who have served as reviewers and those who have been reviewed will be most helpful in determining how to revise the plan.

Summary

The work of developing a plan for peer review of teaching is substantial. It requires articulating values and assumptions regarding teaching in ways that most academics do not routinely do. Additionally, this work demands the development of ways to assess a very complex and critical activity in ways that are not reductionist, yet are practical. Balance and compromise are needed. As has been indicated earlier, however, the discussions for developing peer review plans are fundamental to the health of an academic unit: They bring collective wisdom to bear on the analysis of everyday professional work and implicitly further discussion and understanding of a rationale for practice.

Chapter 4

Roles and Goals of a Peer Review System

Initial clarity about the reasons for engaging in peer review and expectations for the role each person plays in an academic unit are hallmarks of good systems of peer review. This chapter discusses the topics of roles and goals.

Roles

Effective peer review of teaching involves the collaboration of several parties, including the chairperson, colleague being reviewed, and peer reviewer. Each person has a role and a contribution to make in the process. In unionized settings, special adjustments may be needed to comply with contract stipulations on evaluation of teaching.

THE ACADEMIC UNIT LEADER

Whether the champion of a peer review of teaching system is a provost, dean, department chair, or faculty chair of a committee entrusted to its development, this person or group of people are responsible for creating a climate that values peer review. This can only be situated within a climate that values teaching and therefore supports continual efforts to develop and evaluate teaching. Academic leaders can create a supportive climate in several ways.

Assuming intellectual leadership for the effort. Effective academic leaders are knowledgeable about the literature on good teaching, on teaching assessment, and on teaching improvement. They can show faculty that teaching can be analyzed and assessed in valid and reliable ways. They can convene meetings to set up a peer review system that is thorough and informed.

Communicating high expectations for teaching and peer review. Through pronouncements and actions, the academic leader can alert faculty to the serious attitude about teaching that the unit expects. Faculty can be continually informed that peer review is expected and should receive their full attention. Although concerns about how much time goes into effective peer review are important, the leader should communicate a clear sense of the high priority that this function demands.

Making teaching public. Academic leaders can work to ensure that there is ongoing public dialogue about teaching at unit meetings, workshops, and other occasions. The leader can strive to be personally accessible for discussion of teaching issues. Peer review then becomes a natural part of the dialogue.

Providing leadership for integration of peer review across the range of evaluation activities. Administrators can take a big-picture perspective on faculty evaluation and help to ensure that the work of articulating criteria and standards for teaching excellence pervades the individual activities that involve assessment of teaching performance. For example, specifications for nominations for teaching awards should be based on the same principles as other forms of evaluation and can benefit from the same evidence collected through peer review for other purposes. Evaluation of candidates for new faculty positions, similarly, can be based on the principles of teaching effectiveness articulated for other teaching assessment purposes. Chism (2003) discusses the special role of the administrator in the evaluation of teaching.

Providing sufficient resources for peer review. The way in which the academic leader provides leadership in selecting new faculty, allocating rewards, and making assignments clearly indicates a stance on teaching. Leaders should be alert for ways in which they can provide time and resources for serious peer review.

Assisting in the assignment of peers. The academic leader can oversee the process of assigning peer reviewers to assess the work of a given faculty member. This task might be accomplished by delegating it to a faculty committee, by direct nomination or appointment by the leader, or whatever arrangements make sense in the academic unit. The leader can help to ensure fair and helpful reviews by awareness of interpersonal conflicts, philosophical differences, and other conditions among the teaching staff that might get in the way of good peer review.

Taking part in the peer review process. The academic leader within the program unit can set an example by being personally involved in formative peer review, observing faculty in the classroom, reviewing their materials and the like, and providing feedback. The leader plays an important role in summative peer review, setting the tone of the review committee and encouraging it to make decisions based on careful analysis of available information.

Providing guidance to peer reviewers. Within the program unit, the leader can help to arbitrate differences among peers that arise during the review process and can intervene as necessary to help provide perspective on differences among faculty, standards for judgment, and comparisons.

THE COLLEAGUE BEING REVIEWED

Teachers being evaluated can provide important contextual information needed during the peer review process. They can also initiate actions for formative review, inviting peers to provide feedback on course materials, classroom performance, or other aspects of teaching. This self-initiation role is often needed, especially when peer review of teaching plans are nonexistent or are very vague about when peer review activity is to take place. Colleagues are frequently reluctant to offer feedback unless it is invited.

For formative purposes, teachers can provide, during pre-observation conferences or other interchanges, information concerning appropriate materials about the course, the instructional strategies, the level of students taking the course, and other contextual information that can be helpful to the reviewer. Taking a reflective approach is most helpful, as assumptions about teaching are then explored and the why's and how's behind teaching approaches are articulated. Such reflective commentary helps a colleague to understand the rationale for practice and enables a more appropriate response.

The role of the colleague being reviewed for summative purposes is to assemble the best evidence of teaching available and provide additional evidence at the request of the committee. Such evidence includes representative samples of course materials, a chronological record of teaching responsibilities, a list of publications and presentations on teaching, student evaluations of teaching, records of consultations or feedback from sources outside the department, and other required documents of the department or institution in a dossier. Once again, a reflective approach is most helpful in providing a context for thinking about practice decisions and results.

The colleague under review in both formative and summative situations can benefit most by avoiding defensive reactions. When feedback on teaching is regarded as a part of inquiry activities into the nature of facilitating learning rather than as questioning one's personal attributes, peer review activities are considered in a less threatening and more scholarly way. The conversation changes from "What did I do wrong in using small groups?" to "How can small groups be used most effectively in this context to get the desired learning results?"—a significant difference. The colleague under review can also obtain better feedback if he or she practices the habit of checking understanding by summarizing at frequent intervals during a feedback exchange. For example, "I hear you suggesting that I can really improve the functioning of groups if I give the instructions for group work before I ask students to move into groups rather than as they are moving. Is that what you are saying?"

The Peer Reviewer

The peer reviewer can be developer, information gatherer, or judge. In the role of developer, he or she is supportive, assisting the colleague in teaching development and offering suggestions for change and improvement. As information gatherer, the role is one of collecting appropriate information to be used formatively or summatively in the peer review process. As a judge, the peer reviewer evaluates sources of data on teaching that are used for personnel decisions. Ideally, the peer reviewer will play only one of these roles for any given faculty colleague within a given period of time, separating the formative and summative functions.

The role of the reviewer in formative peer review is to gather appropriate information from the colleague during pre-observation conferences or other interchanges concerning appropriate materials about the courses taught, the instructional strategies, the level of students taking the courses, and other contextual information that can be helpful to the reviewer. Once information is gathered, the peer reviewer has the responsibility to view the teaching products or performance in light of the context and make helpful comments and suggestions to the colleague in follow-up sessions. Peer reviewers should be careful to situate their feedback in ways that are helpful and to check with the colleague being reviewed to ensure that the communication of this feedback is being received as intended.

The role of the reviewer in summative peer review is to collect information that the reviewer is best qualified to judge. A review of the literature on the role of colleagues in peer review of teaching (Cohen & McKeachie, 1980) states that peer reviewers are in an ideal position to judge course content and design, materials, and instruments used to assess student achievement. Peers are also the appropriate judges of the products of the scholarship of teaching and the colleague's contributions to teaching development in the department, college, institution, or profession. The peer reviewer should assess the evidence in these areas according to departmental and institutional standards and render fair evaluations based on these standards.

Goals

As has been discussed throughout this sourcebook, it is important to adopt separate procedures for formative and summative peer review. Formative peer review is intended for improvement of the person being reviewed, and the emphasis is on constructive feedback. Summative peer review is intended to be the basis for a personnel decision, such as promotion, tenure, or merit pay, and the emphasis is on making fair judgments. The two approaches should dovetail, however, creating a comprehensive approach.

Centra (1993) discusses the elements necessary for feedback to produce change in faculty behaviors. He speaks of four qualities of feedback that are particularly important: 1) faculty members must gain new knowledge about their teaching—that is, they must learn something that they do not already know; 2) they must trust the source and process that produced the information in order to value it; 3) they must understand what specific actions they can take to make the change that is needed; and 4) they must be motivated to make changes. Centra stresses that intrinsic motivation, connected with an internal drive to do good work rather than to obtain external rewards, is the more powerful motivator for faculty members. He cites scholarship indicating that intrinsic motivation is most likely when faculty members experience the meaningfulness of their work, take responsibility for work outcomes, and see the results of their actions. Bergquist and Phillips (1995), Braskamp and Ory (1994), and Pritchard, Watson, Kelly and Paquin (1998) provide good suggestions on feedback.

FORMATIVE PEER REVIEW: PROVIDING CONSTRUCTIVE FEEDBACK

In providing a colleague with feedback for improvement following a class observation, review of materials, or other peer review activity, it is helpful to consider the following:

- Authentic feedback is built on a relationship of trust, honesty, and genuine concern for the individual. Rivalries, flattery, and condescension get in the way of effective dialogue.
- Descriptive information provides the colleague with concrete details on which decisions for change can be based. It allows the colleague to consider whether the description fits his or her intentions and to make adjustments if not. (Example: "Ninety percent of the class time was devoted to teacher talk" or "The syllabus

never lists the causes of the French Revolution as a topic to be treated.") Additional examples are presented in Table 4.1.

- A focus on behavior rather than personal attributes isolates what can be changed more easily and avoids associating personal blame with problems. (Example: It is better to say "I noticed that the students appeared tired when they did not have a break during the three-hour class" than "You are really inconsiderate.")

- Feedback that is rooted in the needs of the colleague is most helpful. It is responsive to the self-identified questions that the colleague has, to the stage of his or her career, and to the individual's capacity to absorb information and make necessary adjustments. Reviewers should encourage colleagues to identify the questions and concerns that they themselves have. (Example: "In looking over this test, what items do you have uncertainties about?" "Would you like suggestions for redoing the whole format or just changes on specific items?")

- Peer review activities should be followed by prompt feedback. While recall of details is fresh and colleague expectation for response is high, dialogue between the peer reviewer and colleague should occur. It is often helpful to schedule a meeting time for this exchange at the same time when the initial peer review activity is scheduled.

- Checking periodically during a feedback session to hear how comments are being heard and interpreted is helpful. (Example: "Can you summarize the main points I have made about what I saw in the laboratory exercise?")

- If multiple peer reviewers are involved, it is useful to check for agreement on specific observations or advice. (Example: "Did anyone else notice that students' attention levels lagged after the first 15 minutes of lecture?" "Do you find the layout of these handouts confusing?")

- Feedback should be about what a colleague is able to change. Control over action to change is essential. For example, if the heat in the classroom is impairing student performance and there is no other option to change the facility, ways of compensating might be discussed, but the change is not totally within the purview of the instructor, so this point should be regarded as of lesser value than other topics for discussion.

- Feedback that is forward-looking helps the colleague to go beyond the peer review activity. When suggestions for specific change or a plan for development are part of a feedback session, the colleague has identified a practical outcome. (Example: "I would suggest that you limit the content of your overhead transparencies and use a bigger, bolder font so that students stop complaining that they cannot see them or copy them down quickly.")

Table 4.1 Examples of Specific and Descriptive Language for Feedback Purposes

*These examples are followed by improvement suggestions,
if these are appropriate to the function of the review.*

As the time for the end of class neared, students were packing their bags and putting on their gloves, even though the last topic was just introduced.

Suggestion: Early on in a course, establish the expectation that you will take care to end on time and that the students should respect you and others by not creating distractions toward the end of class.

Students were straining to see the small print on the slides even though you told them it was unnecessary for them to copy all the data.

Suggestion: It might be better to redo the slides to include just what data you want the students to note.

In talking about the newspaper report on the observed drug interaction, you became noticeably more animated. Students responded with several questions and comments. In fact, this segment contained the only participation that occurred during the class.

Suggestion: Perhaps added human interest items at planned intervals would enable you to sustain this engagement throughout the session.

As the class broke into groups, the noise level made it hard to hear the instructions that you were issuing.

Suggestion: I have found that it is best to give instruction for the task before asking students to move to groups.

SUMMATIVE PEER REVIEW: RENDERING JUDGMENTS

When peer review of teaching is performed for summative purposes, several guidelines are relevant:

- Reviewers should make sure that they are appropriate judges. If there are conflicts of interest, if the teaching is being done in a specialized area that is unfamiliar to the reviewer, if there are long-standing personality conflicts between the reviewer and the colleague being reviewed or the reviewer and other peers on a review committee, or if there are other compelling reasons why the reviewer cannot do a thorough and fair job, the reviewer should request to be excused from the review.

- Adequate conditions should be available for summative peer review of teaching. If there is an attitude of distrust, insufficient time, or lack of evidence, these must be addressed before a good review is possible. If lead time has been lacking, an extension should be sought. If there are insufficient materials or an absence of the contextual information needed to understand the materials, the missing information should be requested from the colleague under review.

- The review should be based on standards. As emphasized in Chapter 3, to prevent personal preference from prevailing, standards for effective teaching based on institutional, college, or departmental policies should be used in making judgments about teaching. Professional associations often have documents that contain teaching standards as well. Peer reviewers should make sure that they obtain copies of these standards in advance of the review. If they are not available from any of these sources, a discussion of standards is necessary at the start of the review. They should be made explicit so that the basis for the review is articulated.

- Conclusions should be tied to evidence. Statements about the teaching of the colleague should be rooted in the specifics of the documentation that has been provided. (Example: A finding that the instructor lacks content knowledge should be supported by references to some particular mistakes or omissions that have surfaced in the review of materials or classroom performance.)

- Summative peer review conducted at personnel decision-making checkpoints (promotion and tenure, contract extension, merit pay) should be comprehensive and comparative. Unlike formative peer review of teaching, summative review should focus on overall performance. While judgments about this performance should be grounded in specifics, the attempt should be to assess the teaching holistically over an extended period of time and range of conditions, rather than to focus on a given instance. For this purpose, then, isolated findings should not determine the conclusions so much as general patterns. These patterns need to be viewed within the context of the teaching performance of the colleague's peers as well. (Example: Is the involvement in teaching improvement efforts heavier, lighter, or about the same as the involvement of others in these activities within the department? Should it be so, given the context of the department and expectations for the colleague?)

Peer review, whether for formative or summative purposes, should be thoughtfully conducted. Reviewers should have the opportunity to engage in meaningful dialogue with other peers while the process takes place. Reviewers should "prepare themselves to care," being generous of spirit in their critiques, yet trying to isolate specific issues that can be improved or singled out for praise and recognition. A hallmark of an effective review is that the reviewers themselves learn through the process. As they uncover teaching issues for judgment, their conversation should help to illuminate the issues involved. The review should culminate in a written summary that is thorough, grounded in evidence, and clear in its conclusions.

Part II

Resources and Forms

Chapter 5

Peer Review of Course Materials

Course materials are very important in supporting the learning that takes place in a course. They promote in-class learning and are also critical in shaping out-of-class experiences. Students with strong visual learning styles rely heavily on written course materials. The way in which an instructor uses print or digital materials and the content of the materials themselves provide a window on the course philosophy, expectations, scope, and presentation of subject matter. When it comes to assessing the accuracy and adequacy of instructional materials, peers are in an ideal position. Indeed, most writers on peer review see review of course materials as the optimal way in which peers can be involved.

Arguments for the review of course materials include the relative unobtrusiveness of the method: Classrooms do not have to be interrupted in order to do these reviews. Convenience is another factor: Reviews can occur at a time and place suitable to the schedule of the reviewer and do not require special preparations on the part of the teacher being reviewed. Third, the power of disclosure is often quite high: A look at a test can tell much about the level of learning goals in the course, the instructor's perception of what is important, and the instructor's pedagogical style toward the students. Graded tests, written work, or projects can tell all of the above, as well as indicate how an instructor provides feedback to learners and implements an assessment scheme. Finally, reviewers can gain insights into their own teaching through working with sets of questions that enumerate characteristics of effective course materials. Good sets of questions are posed by Braskamp and Ory (1994, pp. 289–290), Keig and Waggoner (1994, pp. 61–62), and Nordstrom (1995, p. 131). Several sets of such questions are contained in the resource materials section of this chapter. In addition, Richlin (2006) includes an extensive selection of well-developed rubrics for assessing various types of course materials in her book. Since course materials are often part of a teaching portfolio, the references in Chapter 9 about portfolios may also be helpful.

For Formative Evaluation

For formative evaluation, use of course materials can enable a mentor or mentor team to see an instructor's philosophy in practice. Regular and thoughtful review of materials can alert mentors to the areas in which a given instructor excels and to areas where improvement can be cultivated. When used in peer dialogue groups, exchanges of materials, such as course syllabi, can promote reflective discussion about the overall goals of the academic unit, ways of effectively motivating and facilitating the success of the students, and the like. Bernstein (2002), Bernstein, Burnett, Goodburn, and Savory (2006), and Hutchings (1995) discuss how conversations stimulated by a course syllabus can lead to powerful examinations of teaching assumptions and practices. In these conversations, ideas can be shared for the enrichment of all, cultivating teaching as community property and intellectual activity.

For Summative Evaluation

When used in summative evaluation, review of course materials is normally conducted to provide one point of information on the instructor's overall effectiveness, compared with others in the academic unit or profession. Often, this work is delegated to one or two peer reviewers, who then write an assessment that becomes part of the final dossier that is reviewed.

The large number of course materials becomes an important issue and potential drawback to this approach. When a review covers several years of work, whole file drawers of course materials might conceivably be at issue. Deciding how to choose representative syllabi, tests, course notes, handouts, computer software, or other materials can be done in several ways. The most frequently used is to ask the faculty member being reviewed to submit a portfolio of materials. One would expect that the teacher would choose those items considered best for summative reviews or perhaps those about which he or she is uncertain for formative reviews. Another method is to make specific requests, based on concerns within the department. For example, if a given course is the first in a sequence for which it is necessary that students build on skills of the prior course, requesting to see a copy of the final exam or course project requirement for that course might be a useful way to determine whether the course is serving its function in the sequence. If the unit is working to cultivate student-centered teaching, the review team might choose to look at the course syllabus for a critical introductory course and review it according to principles of student-centered learning. For summative purposes, it is probably best for certain documents to be specified for review so that all instructors are treated similarly. Such requirements might include, at minimum, the submission of the course syllabus for particular courses of interest (including bibliographies) and the final exam or project format for these courses.

The widespread use of instructional technology has created special considerations for review of course materials. These are discussed in Chapter 7. The review of materials used with special forms of instruction, such as case studies, problem-based learning, and laboratory or field-based instruction, is also presented in Chapter 7.

Materials for Peer Review

Course materials (either print or electronic) that can be the focus of peer review include:

1. Materials that communicate course policy and practices
   - Syllabus
   - Ground rules for discussion
   - Course guides
   - Teaching evaluation instruments
2. Materials that communicate content
   - Course packets
   - Texts
   - Bibliographies
   - Overhead transparencies
   - Handouts
   - Computer simulations, videotapes, and other multimedia supplements
3. Materials that set assignments and assess student performance
   - Tests
   - Project assignment directions, and handouts
   - Classroom exercises (case studies, learning group tasks)
4. Instructor comments on student work
   - Graded papers or tests
   - Journals and email exchanges

Overall Guidelines

It is important to remember that course materials are not the course. Although such materials can be powerful indicators of an instructor's approach, there can also be a gap between what the instructor intends to do as planned on paper and how these intentions are expressed. It is possible (although not too likely) that an instructor with clear and well-organized class handouts can be rude to students and rambling and inaccurate in class. Combining review of course materials with evidence gathered in other ways is necessary to arrive at a full picture.

Understanding the instructor's rationale and the context of the course is important in evaluating course materials. For formative review, instructors may provide this orally in informal discussions with the reviewer. In the case of summative review, this will generally be done in writing as part of the dossier.

Given the specialized nature of many course materials, the peer reviewer may be unfamiliar with the content of specific courses but may still be able to review the basic format, tone, and appropriateness of the materials. It may be necessary to solicit the opinions of others in the field of specialization to review accuracy and currency of content. Fortunately, most documents are available in electronic format and can be sent to reviewers at a distance.

PROCEDURES FOR FORMATIVE EVALUATION OF COURSE MATERIALS

1. Collect a representative sample (across courses and time) and information about the context in which they are used.
2. Prior to any formative review, identify the instructor's questions or concerns so that these can be addressed in your review.
3. Review the materials (instruments for helping to do this are in the resource materials section of this chapter).
4. Within two weeks of conducting the review, schedule a feedback conversation with the instructor about the review. See Chapter 4 for constructive feedback techniques.
5. Remain available for help as issues arise in the future.

PROCEDURES FOR SUMMATIVE EVALUATION OF COURSE MATERIALS

1. Collect a representative sample (across courses and time) of materials and information about the context in which they are used.
2. Identify standards for these materials in the field of study (or at the academic unit or institutional level) or model materials prepared by others in the department.

3. Decide whether certain instruments are to be used and apply them consistently (instruments for helping to do this are in resource materials section of this chapter).
4. Review the materials.
5. Report on the results either by using a narrative approach or by submitting checklists or ratings sheets.

Resource Materials
Peer Review of Course Materials

*It is important that groups using these forms define their standards
for what each of the descriptors means within their context on each item.*

Policies
The Syllabus: The Document Itself

The Course Described by the Document

Course Guidelines, Ground Rules for Discussion, and Other Policy
and/or Procedure Documents

Formative Teaching Evaluation Instruments for Student Feedback

Summative Teaching Evaluation Instruments for Student Feedback

Content
Course Packet and Textbook Content

Course Bibliographies

Overhead Transparencies or Presentation Slides

Course Handouts

Multimedia Course Materials

Assignments
Tests

Class Assignments and Course Exercise Sheets

Instructor Comments
Instructor Comments on Student Work

Peer Review of the Syllabus:
The Document Itself

For formative use: Focus on providing comments.
For summative use: Complete ratings and use comments to explain them.

	Exceeds level of expected qualities	Meets level on all qualities	Meets level on most qualities	Meets level on some qualities	Meets no/few expected qualities
Completeness	5	4	3	2	1

Does the syllabus have each of the following, if relevant?

- Course information

- Instructor information

- Information on course readings

- Goals and objectives of course

- Policies on grading, academic misconduct, late work, absences, safety issues, accommodations for special needs

- Calendar of activities

- Descriptions of assignments and due dates

- Support services available

Comment:

Chism, N.V.N. (2007). *Peer Review of Teaching: A Sourcebook*. Bolton, MA: Anker.

	Exceeds level of expected qualities	Meets level on all qualities	Meets level on most qualities	Meets level on some qualities	Meets no/few expected qualities

Clarity of communication

5   4   3   2   1

- Is the syllabus clear?
- Are rights, responsibilities, and consequences spelled out?
- Is information internally consistent?
- Is information consistent with department or university policy?

Comment:

Appropriateness of tone

5   4   3   2   1

- Does the syllabus further rapport and respect between instructor and students?
- Does it communicate a helpful, positive attitude?
- Is it motivational, nonthreatening?
- Is it inclusive in its language?
- Does it communicate the challenge of the course?

Comment:

Professional appearance

5   4   3   2   1

- Is the syllabus well formatted?
- Are the grammar and spelling correct?
- Is it attractive?

Comment:

Other

Chism, N.V.N. (2007). *Peer Review of Teaching: A Sourcebook*. Bolton, MA: Anker.

Peer Review of the Syllabus:
The Course Described by the Document

For formative use: Focus on providing comments.
For summative use: Complete ratings and use comments to explain them.

	Exceeds level of expected qualities	Meets level on all qualities	Meets level on most qualities	Meets level on some qualities	Meets no/few expected qualities

Currency of content

| | 5 | 4 | 3 | 2 | 1 |

- Does this course portray the current state of the field in this area?

- Does it use readings or other materials that reflect the latest scholarship?

Comment:

Fit within the curriculum

| | 5 | 4 | 3 | 2 | 1 |

- Does the course fulfill expectations of the academic unit for content and process skills needed for subsequent courses?

- Does it evidence inclusiveness with respect to culture and ability?

- Does it match the catalog description and expected overall fit within the curriculum of the institution?

- Does it duplicate other courses or is it undesirably idiosyncratic to one topic area or school of thinking?

Comment:

Level of challenge

| | 5 | 4 | 3 | 2 | 1 |

- Does the course require students to do an appropriate amount of reading and other assignments?

- Are these at an appropriate level of challenge?

Comment:

Chism, N.V.N. (2007). *Peer Review of Teaching: A Sourcebook*. Bolton, MA: Anker.

	Exceeds level of expected qualities	Meets level on all qualities	Meets level on most qualities	Meets level on some qualities	Meets no/few expected qualities

Pacing

5   4   3   2   1

- Is the course calendar realistic?
- Has the instructor selected a reasonable amount of content for the time allotted?
- Are the due dates for assignments distributed well?

Comment:

Testing and grading

5   4   3   2   1

- Do students receive frequent feedback?
- Are grading policies fair and appropriate for the goals?

Comment:

Student-centeredness

5   4   3   2   1

- Do office hours or other information portray that the instructor is accessible for help?
- Are other resources available to the student?
- Do activities show a concern for active student engagement?

Comment:

Other

Chism, N.V.N. (2007). *Peer Review of Teaching: A Sourcebook.* Bolton, MA: Anker.

Peer Review of Course Guidelines, Ground Rules for Discussion, and Other Policy and/or Procedure Documents

For formative use: Focus on providing comments.
For summative use: Complete ratings and use comments to explain them.

	Exceeds level of expected qualities	Meets level on all qualities	Meets level on most qualities	Meets level on some qualities	Meets no/few expected qualities

Clarity of communication   5   4   3   2   1

- Is the rationale clear?

- Are rights, responsibilities, and consequences spelled out?

- Is information internally consistent?

- Is information consistent with department or university policy?

Comment:

Appropriateness of tone   5   4   3   2   1

- Do the documents further the rapport between instructor and students?

- Are they motivational, nonthreatening?

- Do they include all groups?

Comment:

Instructional value   5   4   3   2   1

- Are the documents consistent with course goals and content?

- Do they suggest helpful ways of achieving success?

Comment:

Professional appearance   5   4   3   2   1

- Are the documents well formatted?

- Are the grammar and spelling correct?

Comment:

Other

Chism, N.V.N. (2007). *Peer Review of Teaching: A Sourcebook*. Bolton, MA: Anker.

Peer Review of Formative Teaching Evaluation Instruments for Student Feedback

(instruments that suggest possible improvements, intended for instructor's own use)

For formative use: Focus on providing comments.
For summative use: Complete ratings and use comments to explain them.

	Exceeds level of expected qualities	Meets level on all qualities	Meets level on most qualities	Meets level on some qualities	Meets no/few expected qualities

Allows students to provide detailed comments

- Has open-ended items and sufficient writing space.

	5	4	3	2	1

Comment:

Is tailored to goals and practices of the course

- Asks about specific activities, handouts, content coverage, etc.

	5	4	3	2	1

Comment:

Asks students for recommendations for change

- Prompts students to think about specific issues such as textbook, laboratories, and what would work better.

	5	4	3	2	1

Comment:

Provides opportunities for unsolicited data

- Asks: "Are there any other thoughts?"

	5	4	3	2	1

Comment:

Chism, N.V.N. (2007). *Peer Review of Teaching: A Sourcebook.* Bolton, MA: Anker.

Other

Peer Review of Summative Teaching Evaluation
Instruments for Student Feedback

(intended primarily for decision-making to provide comparative data in summary form)

For formative use: Focus on providing comments.
For summative use: Complete ratings and use comments to explain them.

Yes   No   Results can be easily summarized
(Uses numbers that can be averaged, text categories that
can be quickly analyzed for patterns)

Yes   No   Provides comparison data
(Expected norms or average scores of other instructors
using this instrument are available)

Yes   No   Is valid and reliable
(Focuses on what is to be measured, has history
of consistent results)

Yes   No   Asks for global information
(Taps into broad dimensions of teaching, rather
than course-specific issues)

Yes   No   Is clear
(Provides explicit directions for students and
unambiguous items)

Overall evaluation form rating:

Satisfactory   **Unsuitable for use**

Chism, N.V.N. (2007). *Peer Review of Teaching: A Sourcebook.* Bolton, MA: Anker.

Peer Review of Course Packet and Textbook Content

For formative use: Focus on providing comments.
For summative use: Complete ratings and use comments to explain them.

	Excellent	Very Good	Good	Fair	Poor
Match with goals of course Comment:	5	4	3	2	1
Accuracy of content Comment:	5	4	3	2	1
Currency of content Comment:	5	4	3	2	1
Multiple viewpoints presented Comment:	5	4	3	2	1
Interest level Comment:	5	4	3	2	1
Appropriateness of reading level Comment:	5	4	3	2	1
Attractiveness Comment:	5	4	3	2	1
Appropriateness of amount of reading Comment:	5	4	3	2	1
Clarity of organization Comment:	5	4	3	2	1
User friendliness Comment:	5	4	3	2	1
Reputation and expertise of authors Comment:	5	4	3	2	1
Fair use of copyright Comment:	5	4	3	2	1

Other

Chism, N.V.N. (2007). *Peer Review of Teaching: A Sourcebook.* Bolton, MA: Anker.

Peer Review of Course Bibliographies

For formative use: Focus on providing comments.
For summative use: Complete ratings and use comments to explain them.

	Excellent	Very Good	Good	Fair	Poor
Currency of works listed Comment:	5	4	3	2	1
Importance of works cited Comment:	5	4	3	2	1
Thoroughness of bibliography Comment:	5	4	3	2	1
Completeness of citations Comment:	5	4	3	2	1
If annotated, usefulness of summaries Comment:	5	4	3	2	1
Appropriateness for course Comment:	5	4	3	2	1
Appropriateness for level of student Comment:	5	4	3	2	1
Relationship to course content Comment:	5	4	3	2	1

Other

Chism, N.V.N. (2007). *Peer Review of Teaching: A Sourcebook*. Bolton, MA: Anker.

Peer Review of Overhead Transparencies or Presentation Slides

For formative use: Focus on providing comments.
For summative use: Complete ratings and use comments to explain them.

	Excellent	Very Good	Good	Fair	Poor
Enhances representation of course content Comment:	5	4	3	2	1
Expresses content clearly Comment:	5	4	3	2	1
Presents material legibly Comment:	5	4	3	2	1
Displays appropriate amounts of material Comment:	5	4	3	2	1
Contains accurate content Comment:	5	4	3	2	1
Shows evidence of proofreading Comment:	5	4	3	2	1

Other

Chism, N.V.N. (2007). *Peer Review of Teaching: A Sourcebook.* Bolton, MA: Anker.

Peer Review of Course Handouts

For formative use: Focus on providing comments.
For summative use: Complete ratings and use comments to explain them.

	Excellent	Very Good	Good	Fair	Poor
Supplements course content Comment:	5	4	3	2	1
Contains accurate content Comment:	5	4	3	2	1
Shows evidence of proofreading Comment:	5	4	3	2	1
Is at appropriate reading level Comment:	5	4	3	2	1
Is at adequate level of detail Comment:	5	4	3	2	1
Demonstrates instructional skills Comment:	5	4	3	2	1
Shows creativity (if applicable) Comment:	5	4	3	2	1

Other

Chism, N.V.N. (2007). *Peer Review of Teaching: A Sourcebook.* Bolton, MA: Anker.

Peer Review of Multimedia Course Materials

(see also Chapter 7 forms)

For formative use: Focus on providing comments.
For summative use: Complete ratings and use comments to explain them.

1. Overall Items

	Excellent	Very Good	Good	Fair	Poor
Match with goals of course Comment:	5	4	3	2	1
Accuracy of content Comment:	5	4	3	2	1
Currency of content Comment:	5	4	3	2	1
Production quality Comment:	5	4	3	2	1
Interest level Comment:	5	4	3	2	1
Attractiveness Comment:	5	4	3	2	1
Appropriateness of length Comment:	5	4	3	2	1
Appropriate level of difficulty Comment:	5	4	3	2	1
Clarity of organization Comment:	5	4	3	2	1
User friendliness Comment:	5	4	3	2	1

Chism, N.V.N. (2007). *Peer Review of Teaching: A Sourcebook*. Bolton, MA: Anker.

2. Optional Items (if applicable)

	Excellent	Very Good	Good	Fair	Poor
Permits interactivity Comment:	5	4	3	2	1
Permits self-pacing Comment:	5	4	3	2	1
Provides branching options Comment:	5	4	3	2	1
Provides user feedback Comment:	5	4	3	2	1
Provides accommodations for students with special needs Comment:	5	4	3	2	1

Other

Chism, N.V.N. (2007). *Peer Review of Teaching: A Sourcebook*. Bolton, MA: Anker.

Peer Review of Tests

For formative use, focus on providing comments.
For summative use, complete ratings and use comments to explain them.

	Excellent	Very Good	Good	Fair	Poor
Clarity of directions Comment:	5	4	3	2	1
Match of content to course goals Comment:	5	4	3	2	1
Clarity of items Comment:	5	4	3	2	1
Appropriate level of challenge Comment:	5	4	3	2	1
Inclusion of higher order thinking Comment:	5	4	3	2	1
Organization of content Comment:	5	4	3	2	1
Legibility and layout Comment:	5	4	3	2	1
Evidence of proofreading Comment:	5	4	3	2	1
Appropriateness of length Comment:	5	4	3	2	1

Other

Chism, N.V.N. (2007). *Peer Review of Teaching: A Sourcebook.* Bolton, MA: Anker.

Peer Review of Class Assignments and Course Exercise Sheets

For formative use: Focus on providing comments.
For summative use: Complete ratings and use comments to explain them.

	Excellent	Very Good	Good	Fair	Poor
Supplements course content Comment:	5	4	3	2	1
Provides clear directions Comment:	5	4	3	2	1
Encourages meaningful learning experiences Comment:	5	4	3	2	1
Is at appropriate level of challenge Comment:	5	4	3	2	1
Outlines assessment method Comment:	5	4	3	2	1
Clearly states purpose Comment:	5	4	3	2	1
Demonstrates instructor creativity Comment:	5	4	3	2	1
Promotes student engagement Comment:	5	4	3	2	1
Provides adequate time and resources for completion Comment:	5	4	3	2	1

Other

Chism, N.V.N. (2007). *Peer Review of Teaching: A Sourcebook.* Bolton, MA: Anker.

Peer Review of Instructor Comments on Student Work

For formative use: Focus on providing comments.
For summative use: Complete ratings and use comments to explain them.

	Excellent	Very Good	Good	Fair	Poor
Feedback is clear	5	4	3	2	1
Comment:					
Feedback is legible	5	4	3	2	1
Comment:					
Feedback is supportive of student efforts	5	4	3	2	1
Comment:					
Constructive suggestions are provided	5	4	3	2	1
Comment:					
Comments show consistency	5	4	3	2	1
Comment:					
Comments are motivational toward further progress	5	4	3	2	1
Comment:					
Comments show appropriate expectations for level of student	5	4	3	2	1
Comment:					
Comments display content accuracy	5	4	3	2	1
Comment:					
Amount of feedback is appropriate	5	4	3	2	1
Comment:					

Other

Chism, N.V.N. (2007). *Peer Review of Teaching: A Sourcebook*. Bolton, MA: Anker.

Chapter 6

Classroom Observation

Classroom observation is perhaps the most familiar form of peer review. Unfortunately, it is the most prone to reliability problems, often the result when uninformed peers make brief visits and report from the perspective of their own biases. The evaluation literature makes it clear that the consistent presence of students in the classroom makes them a better source of information about such things as an instructor's approach, fairness, clarity of explanations, and the like. Students, however, cannot be expected to be accurate judges of such areas as the subject matter competency of the instructor or the instructor's use of teaching strategies current to the discipline. For these purposes, peer review is important. The peer's experiential base and credibility with the instructor are also assets for this form of evaluation. Some insight on these aspects of teaching can be obtained through classroom observation. With proper understanding of how to observe classes, peers can use this method to provide data points for improvement and decision-making.

An advantage of classroom observation by peers is that the peers' own development may be fostered through the ideas obtained from watching a colleague. Beckman (2004) speaks to this benefit in his study of peer observation in clinical settings. Reciprocal classroom observations are a strategy employed in many faculty development programs, such as the New Jersey Master Teacher Program (Golin, 1990). A classic account of reciprocal peer classroom observation is provided by Peter Elbow in his 1980 essay "One-to-One Faculty Development." In some cases, peer classroom observation is complemented by other methods, such as student interviewing or dialogue groups, for the purposes of mutual faculty development.

Overall Guidelines

1. It cannot be assumed that peer reviewers are skilled classroom observers. Academic units using peer classroom observation should engage potential reviewers in activities designed to explore observational goals and methods. They can watch videotapes together to generate ideas on what is important to look for, they can read and react to each other's narrative reports of the same videotaped class, they can use and compare ratings on a departmental rating form for classroom observation. A teaching consultant can lead training on classroom observation, suggesting and offering practice in various ways of approaching this task. Efforts on preparing faculty to do classroom observations increase reliability of the results.

2. A single classroom observation by one rater is not a reliable indicator of teaching quality. Lewis (2001), for example, recommends that classroom observations be conducted at least three times to establish reliability for summative evaluation purposes. Muchinsky (1995) recommends that two reviewers must observe at least twice during the offering of a course. Arreola (2007) is even more stringent in his recommendation, suggesting that a peer team of three or four reviewers observe eight to ten classes of a given instructor. The viewpoints of multiple raters should be presented when possible.

3. Pre-observation information is necessary to provide contextual information about the course, instructor, and students. It is best to obtain this face to face, but a telephone conversation or written description from the course instructor can be used if there are no opportunities for a meeting. Information that might be obtained is listed in the resource materials section of this chapter.

4. During the classroom observation, a variety of approaches can be used to focus the observation. These include a holistic approach followed by a narrative report, an analytical approach that uses a checklist or rating form to assess specific aspects of the class, videotaping, or more specialized systems such as teacher behavior coding instruments or mapping techniques. Millis (2006) provides a helpful model for designing or revising such instruments. An adaptation of her approach aimed at helping groups to develop an observation form is included in the resources section of this chapter.

5. The observer should try to be as unobtrusive as possible. The instructor might refer to the presence of the observer at the beginning of class if this seems necessary but should refrain from making explanatory comments that might affect

the behavior of the students. If the reviewer is not staying for the whole class, the instructor should know this in advance.

6. To allow the instructor and class to relax into typical patterns of behavior, observing over a substantial amount of time is necessary. In the case of a one-hour class, the entire class should be observed. For longer classes, a one-hour or longer segment can be chosen, based on the information gathered during the pre-observation stage as to which segment would be most appropriate.

7. Following the observation, the observer should complete the notes, forms, or other reports while the information is fresh.

Procedures for Class Observation in the Formative Evaluation of Classroom Teaching

1. During the pre-observation conference, information on the instructor's concerns and results of prior feedback should help focus the evaluation. The instructor may, for example, ask the observer to pay particular attention to discussion-leading skills.

2. The approach used by the observer should permit the gathering of specific information so that concrete details and suggestions can be recorded for later review with the instructor. Extensive notes should be taken since a rich, descriptive record will be helpful in debriefing.

3. Personal feedback after the observation is essential. The peer and instructor should debrief the class session, with each providing reflections. The observer should provide constructive feedback with the goal of helping the instructor to map a strategy for improvement.

4. The observer should be available for follow-up observations or conversations with the instructor as the improvement plan is implemented.

Keig and Waggoner (1994, p. 95), summarizing the characteristics of effective programs of collaborative peer observation in place at several institutions, list other recommendations for using classroom observation in formative evaluation of teaching:

- Programs should be built on the premise [of improvement] . . . and should not be considered remedial.
- Faculty participation should be voluntary.
- The observed teacher and the observer should be trusted and respected by each other.
- Classroom visits should be reciprocal (a faculty member should be, in turn, observed and observer) . . .
- Observations should occur by invitation only (there should be no surprise visits).

- Participants should determine in advance what other procedures, if any, are to be employed in assessing teaching performance.
- The lines of communication between the observed faculty member and the observer should be open (feedback should be both candid and tactful).
- A balance between praise and constructive criticism should guide the feedback process.
- Results should be kept strictly confidential and apart from the summative evaluation.

PROCEDURES FOR CLASSROOM OBSERVATION FOR THE SUMMATIVE EVALUATION OF CLASSROOM TEACHING

1. When information from a classroom observation is to be used summatively, particular care should be taken to assure the reliability of the observation. Guidelines for how the observer should be chosen, how many observations should occur, how long the observations should last, and what approach is used to gather and report data should be agreed upon in the department and followed consistently.
2. A set of criteria that the department determines to be characteristic of good classroom teaching should be developed and used to focus classroom observations.
3. The approach used by the observer should permit the gathering of information that is representative of the instructor's overall teaching and reported in a format that enables it to be compared with information from other instructors.
4. The report should provide information on the process used to gather feedback and the context in which the observations took place.

Useful advice for observing classroom teaching is provided in several guides including Millis (1992, 2006) and Sorcinelli (1984). Various checklists and ratings forms have been developed to assist peers with classroom observation. In general, they are based on characteristics of effective teaching that have been consistently identified in the literature, such as teacher organization, content knowledge, enthusiasm, rapport with students, and clarity. These methods include:

- Taking field notes
- Completing ratings forms
- Using teacher behavioral assessment systems

Samples of instruments and reporting formats are contained in the resource materials section of this chapter.

Resource Materials

Classroom Observation

Procedures for Developing an Observation Instrument

Preparation for Observation

The Narrative Log

Classroom Observation Rating Forms
    Template: Classroom Observation Rating Form
    Narrative Prompt Forms
    Checklist Forms
    Scaled Rating Forms

Teacher Behavior Systems

Procedures for Developing an Observation Instrument

Millis (2006) describes a participative approach to developing a system for peer observation of teaching. The following approach is adapted from her ideas.

The development group should consist of a group of faculty members who have experience with the type of teaching that will be observed. Ideally, a facilitator—perhaps a consultant from the campus teaching and learning center or other unit charged with instructional development—might help the group through the process, but the group may also self-facilitate.

The first task is the selection of aspects of teaching that are to be assessed through observation. These should be things that can be seen through observation, as opposed to things for which other approaches would be better sources of evidence. For example, judging how well an instructor gives feedback on written work would best be determined by looking at graded work rather than classroom observation, but judging how an instructor provides verbal feedback to learners as they work can be observed in a live setting. Therefore, the first question a group should ask is:

> *What aspects of teaching will we observe? [brainstorm and prioritize]*

It is recommended the group identify only four to six main categories of teaching performance, with subtasks itemized within these. Ideas may be gleaned from the categories listed in the narrative form and checklist form templates later in this section.

Once these categories are identified, Millis's procedure is helpful for getting group input on the questions one might ask an observer to comment on in the instructional setting:

> *What questions might we ask about the performance within this aspect of teaching?*
> *[brainstorm for each aspect successively]*

For example, if the category is "Instructional Methods," observers might be asked to comment on such questions as: What instructional approach(es) are being used in the setting? Are they appropriate for the type of class, level of student, and goals for learning? To generate a list of these questions and achieve consensus across the group, Millis suggests that subgroups of the development team each generate such questions independently and then compare the lists to produce a final list. The questions should focus on those aspects of instructional performance that the group thinks are most critical to learning and that can

Chism, N.V.N. (2007*). Peer Review of Teaching: A Sourceb*ook. Bolton, MA: Anker.

be observed in a live setting. The group might include guiding questions for the observer to help him or her judge from specific examples whether a more general performance pattern is present. For instance, within the category of "Establishes Rapport with Students," a guiding question might be: Does the instructor know students' names?

Once a list of categories, subtopics, questions, and guiding questions are generated, the group needs to decide whether a narrative or structured form is desirable and format the questions into a tool that will be piloted by peers and then revised for use. A policy document that details the particulars of how the form should be used (formatively, summatively, how often, with which faculty, etc.) should accompany the form.

Chism, N.V.N. (2007). *Peer Review of Teaching: A Sourcebook*. Bolton, MA: Anker.

Preparation for Observation

In order for the peer reviewer to situate a classroom observation within the context of the total course and the instructor's development, a conference should be scheduled. Sometimes, this may be an extended discussion, while at other times, a note or telephone conversation may have to suffice. The following form provides examples of the kinds of information that might be sought from the instructor before a classroom observation takes place.

Pre-observation Conference Form

Prior to the scheduled observation, the peer reviewer might use the following form (or an adaptation of the form) to structure the discussion of the teaching context with the instructor to be reviewed. Information can focus on class goals, students, learning activities, and particular teaching style. The peer reviewer should request that the instructor bring a copy of the syllabus, text, and any pertinent material to help the reviewer understand the content and cognitive level of the course.

Instructor:_____ Date:_____ Time:_____

Course Number:_____Course Title: _____

Course Meeting Time:_____ Level of Students: _____

1. What are the goals for the class that I will observe?
2. What are your plans for achieving these goals?
3. What teaching/learning activities will take place?
4. What have students been asked to do in preparation for this class?
5. Will this class be typical of your teaching style? If not, why?
6. What would you like me to focus on during the observation? (for formative review)
7. Are there other things that I should be aware of prior to the observation?
8. Logistics: Confirm time and place, where observer should sit, whether observer is expected to interact or not, how long observer will stay, and the like.

Chism, N.V.N. (2007). *Peer Review of Teaching: A Sourceb*ook. Bolton, MA: Anker.

The Narrative Log

The narrative log, used mainly for formative purposes, should describe verbal and non-verbal behavior, emphasizing what the reviewer sees rather than the reviewer's judgment. (Some reviewers use a double-entry format, shown on the next page, that lists descriptive material on the right of the page and reflections on the left.) It is particularly useful to record times when a behavior or activity occurred so that the structure of the class can be placed into context and the amount of time spent on certain activities can be assessed.

Narrative logs are used to help instructors review a class after it has occurred. They can stimulate recall and freeze the class in time for the purpose of examination. During a post-observation conference, the log can be used to trigger the instructor's consideration of fit of actions to goals, student learning issues, alternate ways that situations could have been handled, and the like. A much more convenient way of capturing such information is to use videotape; however, the presence of a camera in the classroom can cause uneasiness for both the instructor and students, at least at first. Ways to use videotape effectively are summarized by Keig and Waggoner (1994).

Some topics that can focus the narrative log include:

- What is the instructor speaking about?
- What specific comments are being made?
- What types of questions are being asked?
- How are classroom learning activities organized? (Create a chart if necessary.)
- What is the level of student interaction?
- What teaching strategies are being used?
- What are your impressions of what is being observed? (Keep separate from the observation.)

Chism, N.V.N. (2007). *Peer Review of Teaching: A Sourcebook.* Bolton, MA: Anker.

Example of a Portion of a Double-Entry Narrative Log

Organized start, good student rapport	1:21	Dr. Smith arrives early and sets out materials to be used, aligns the overhead projector and tests it, and begins to greet students as they arrive. Three students talk with her during this time, two apparently asking for clarification of an assignment and one sharing an article with her. She reacts with great enthusiasm and surprise, conversing with the student about possible mutual acquaintances and experiences. At the bell time, all but three students are present and seated.
Nice atmosphere. Clear about goals for class. Appreciates students' contributions but is good at displacing off-topic statement. Only male students participate at this time. Evidence that students have read prior to class. Too much time spent setting up class? Class combines student and instructor choice of direction.	1:30	Dr. Smith begins with a joke about something in the morning's news. She then reviews what had happened in the last class and states the objectives of this class, which she phrases as: to be able to use learning style research in classroom instruction. She asks the students if they would like to state their special interests in this topic, based on their advanced reading. The first student to respond says that he is skeptical about the ability of Myers-Briggs instruments to accurately describe people. Dr. Smith does not respond directly, but writes on the board "accuracy of instruments" as a topic to be dealt with later. The next student feeds off the previous student's comment about the Myers-Briggs, talking about a job interview when it was used. Dr. Smith refocuses the topic by repeating, "What things would you like to talk about today with respect to classroom use?" Several students list ideas, which Smith summarizes and posts as "variety of things being assessed by learning style theorists," "match between instructional style and learning style," and "association of learning style and cultural background." Smith says that the discussion will be structured around these topics as well as four that she adds. This process has consumed seven minutes of class time.

Chism, N.V.N. (2007). *Peer Review of Teaching: A Sourcebook*. Bolton, MA: Anker.

Classroom Observation Rating Forms

A variety of pre-constructed forms are available for the rating of classroom instruction by peer observers. These range from checklists of behaviors to higher inference forms that ask for the observer's assessment of the quality of the teaching. Some instruments are general in nature and intended for use in a traditional classroom setting where lecture-discussion is the format. Other instruments are tailored to specific settings, such as the studio or laboratory or to specific learning formats, such as collaborative learning. Since it is important that the rating form match the context of the teaching, this resource materials section will illustrate general formats for forms and present a list of items that can be used to design a form for a particular setting.

FORMAT CONSIDERATIONS

Each form should contain course information, directions for completing the form, and items to be completed.

Course information. The form should contain specific information about the course and observation. For an example, see the template that follows.

Directions. The form should contain directions for reviewers. For an example, see the template that follows.

Chism, N.V.N. (2007). *Peer Review of Teaching: A Sourcebook.* Bolton, MA: Anker.

Template: Classroom Observation Rating Form

Instructor:_____ Date:_____ Time:_____

Course Number:_____ Course Title:_____

Course Meeting Time:_____ Level of Students: _____

Number of Students Present:_____ Reviewer: _____

Directions

For formative peer review use: Focus on providing comments.

For summative peer review use: Complete ratings and use comments to explain them.

Ratings Scale

5 = Extremely effective

4 = Effective

3 = Somewhat effective

2 = Inconsistently effective

1 = Not at all effective

Item Formats

The items that the rater will use are listed next. These may be in the following formats:

- Narrative prompt forms
- Checklists with or without comments
- Scaled rating forms with or without comments

Examples are provided on the following pages.

Chism, N.V.N. (2007). *Peer Review of Teaching: A Sourcebook*. Bolton, MA: Anker.

Narrative Prompt Forms

Narrative prompt forms focus on pre-specified target areas and call for extended comment incorporating the combined description and judgment of the reviewer. For example:

- *Teacher organization.* Comment on the extent to which the teacher made the class plan explicit, followed the plan, had the materials needed for the class, showed evidence of having prepared the content, and the like.

Examples of Prompts in Specific Areas of Instruction

- *Variety and pacing of instruction.* Comment on the extent to which the teacher employed a variety of instructional strategies and paced the class for interest and accomplishment of the goals.
- *Content knowledge.* Comment on the importance, currency, and accuracy of the content presented by the instructor.
- *Presentation skills.* Comment on the instructor's voice, tone, fluency, eye contact, rate of speech, gestures, use of space.
- *Teacher-student rapport.* Comment on the verbal interaction present in class, the extent to which the teacher welcomed and appreciated student discussion, the teacher's openness to class suggestions, and his or her interpersonal skills.
- *Clarity.* Comment on the extent to which the teacher uses examples, is clear with explanations or answers to student questions, defines new terms or concepts.

Examples of General Prompts

- What things went well for this instructor and/or the class?
- What things did not go so well during this particular class?
- What specific suggestions for improvement do you have?
- What things did you learn in the pre- or post-observation conference that influenced your observation and feedback?
- How does this instructor compare with others in the department?

Chism, N.V.N. (2007). *Peer Review of Teaching: A Sourcebook.* Bolton, MA: Anker.

Checklist Forms

Checklist forms, with or without space for comments, focus on description (the presence or absence of certain characteristics) and emphasize low inference items. Items are chosen in accordance with the instructional values of the instructor's unit. The measures can be simply "yes" or "no" or can be measures of frequency, such as "Always, Often, Sometimes, Never." Comments can be used by the reviewer to explain the rationale for choosing the rating or for providing additional information. For example:

The instructor states the objectives of the class.   _____ Yes   _____ No
Comment:

Possible Items for Checklist Forms *(lower inference items)*

Instructor organization
- The instructor arrives to class on time.
- The instructor states the relation of the class to the previous one.
- The instructor locates class materials as they are needed.
- The instructor knows how to use the educational technology needed for the class.
- The instructor posts class goals or objectives on the board or overhead.
- The instructor posts or verbally provides an outline of the organization of the class.
- The instructor makes transitional statements between class segments.
- The instructor follows the preset structure.
- The instructor conveys the purpose of each class activity.
- The instructor summarizes periodically and at the end of class.

Variety and pacing of instruction
- More than one form of instruction is used.
- During discussion, the instructor pauses after asking questions.
- The instructor accepts student responses.
- The instructor draws nonparticipating students into the discussion.
- The instructor prevents specific students from dominating the discussion.
- The instructor helps students extend their responses.
- The instructor maps the direction of the discussion.
- The instructor mediates conflict or differences of opinion.
- The instructor demonstrates active listening techniques.
- The instructor provides explicit directions for active learning tasks.

Chism, N.V.N. (2007). *Peer Review of Teaching: A Sourcebook.* Bolton, MA: Anker.

- The instructor allows enough time to complete active learning tasks, such as group work.
- The instructor specifies how active learning tasks will be evaluated.
- The instructor is able to complete the topics scheduled for the class.
- The instructor provides time for students to practice.

Content knowledge

- The instructor's statements are accurate according to the standards of the field.
- The instructor incorporates current research in the field.
- The instructor identifies sources, perspectives, and authorities in the field.
- The instructor communicates the reasoning process behind operations or concepts.

Presentation skills

- The instructor's voice is audible.
- The instructor varies the tone and pitch of voice for emphasis and interest.
- The instructor avoids distracting mannerisms.
- The instructor maintains eye contact throughout the class.
- The instructor avoids extended reading from notes or texts.
- The instructor speaks at a pace that allows students to take notes.

Rapport with students

- The instructor addresses students by name.
- The instructor attends to student comprehension or puzzlement.
- The instructor provides feedback at given intervals.
- The instructor uses positive reinforcement.
- The instructor incorporates student ideas into the class.

Clarity

- The instructor defines new terms or concepts.
- The instructor elaborates or repeats complex information.
- The instructor uses examples to explain content.
- The instructor makes explicit statements drawing student attention to certain ideas.
- The instructor pauses during explanations to allow students to ask questions.

Chism, N.V.N. (2007). *Peer Review of Teaching: A Sourcebook*. Bolton, MA: Anker.

Scaled Rating Forms

Rating forms with scales and with or without space for comments focus on higher inference evaluation of specific behaviors. Usually a 5-point scale with specific anchor words such as "Strongly agree/Strongly disagree, Effective/Ineffective, Excellent/Poor" is used. Arreola (2007) cautions that standards of performance be identified (e.g., "The syllabus contains the following items:" etc.) so that reviewers are rating the same thing, and labels on the rating scale are related to the criteria to be evaluated. He notes that interior points of the rating scale should be labeled as well as end points. Others would argue that such precision is cumbersome and ignores the contextual differences between settings. For example, one department might expect a bibliography to be an essential part of a good syllabus, while less print-oriented departments might not. Within a given context, however, it is important that reviewers have some common understanding of what constitutes "Excellent" as opposed to "Very good," "Fair," and the like.

Comments can go below each item, in spaces to the right or left of the item, or at the end of the form. When one form is used for a variety of situations, the rating N/A is provided if certain specific behaviors are not applicable to the setting that is being observed. Illustration:

The instructor is well prepared for class	Extremely	Very well	Adequately	Inconsistently	Not at all		Comment
	5	4	3	2	1	N/A	

Sometimes, such instruments give behavioral indicators of general characteristics in order to increase the likelihood that raters will be attending to the same characteristics. In the above item, for example, the following might be included:

	Exceeds level of expected qualities	Meets level on all qualities	Meets level on most qualities	Meets level on some qualities	Meets no/few expected qualities
The instructor is well prepared for class. (Arrives and starts promptly, has all materials ready and in order, has an articulated class plan, shows content preparation.)	5	4	3	2	1

Chism, N.V.N. (2007). *Peer Review of Teaching: A Sourcebook*. Bolton, MA: Anker.

Possible Items for Scaled Ratings Forms *(higher inference items involving values)*

Teacher organization

- The instructor is well prepared for class.
- The objectives of the class are clearly stated.
- The instructor uses class time efficiently.
- The learning activities are well organized.
- The class remains focused on its objectives.

Instructional strategies

- The instructor's choice of teaching techniques is appropriate for the goals.
- The instructor has good questioning skills.
- The instructor raises stimulating and challenging questions.
- The instructor mediates discussion well.
- The class schedule proceeds at an appropriate pace.
- The instructor uses multimedia effectively.
- Board work is legible and organized.
- Course handouts are used effectively.
- The instructor provides clear directions for group work or other forms of active learning.
- The instructor facilitates group work well.
- The instructor helps students to learn from each other.
- The instructor helps students apply theory to solve problems.
- The instructor effectively holds class attention.
- The instructor provides an effective range of challenges.

Instruction in laboratories, studios, or field settings

- Experiments/exercises are well chosen and well organized.
- Procedures/techniques are clearly explained/demonstrated.
- The instructor is thoroughly familiar with experiments/exercises.
- The instructor is thoroughly familiar with equipment/tools used.
- Assistance is always available during experiments/exercises.
- Experiments/exercises are important supplements to the course.
- Experiments/exercises develop important skills.
- Experiments/exercises are of appropriate length.
- Experiments/exercises are of appropriate level of difficulty.
- Experiments/exercises help to develop confidence in the subject area.
- The instructor provides aid with interpretation of data.
- The instructor's emphasis on safety is evident.

Chism, N.V.N. (2007). *Peer Review of Teaching: A Sourcebook.* Bolton, MA: Anker.

- Criticism of procedures/techniques is constructive.
- The instructor works well with students and other parties in the setting.
- Clinical or field experiences are realistic.

Content knowledge
- The instructor is knowledgeable about the subject matter.
- The instructor is confident in explaining the subject matter.
- The instructor pitches instruction to an appropriate level.
- The instructor uses a variety of illustrations to explain content.
- The instructor provides for sufficient content detail.
- The instructor focuses on important content in the field.
- The instructor demonstrates intellectual curiosity toward new ideas or perspectives.
- The instructor incorporates views of women and minorities.
- The instructor corrects bias in assigned materials.

Presentation skills
- The instructor is an effective speaker.
- The instructor employs an appropriate rate of speech.
- The instructor uses classroom space well.
- The instructor is enthusiastic about the subject matter.
- The instructor makes the subject matter interesting.
- The instructor's command of English is adequate.

Rapport with students
- The instructor welcomes student participation.
- The instructor models good listening habits.
- The instructor motivates students.
- The instructor stimulates interest in the course subject(s).
- The instructor responds well to student differences.
- The instructor demonstrates a sense of humor.
- The instructor uses effective classroom management techniques.
- The instructor demonstrates flexibility in responding to student concerns or interests.
- The instructor welcomes multiple perspectives.
- The instructor anticipates student problems.
- The instructor treats students impartially.
- The instructor respects constructive criticism.

Chism, N.V.N. (2007). *Peer Review of Teaching: A Sourcebook.* Bolton, MA: Anker.

- The instructor celebrates diversity and avoids statements that demean particular groups.
- The instructor is able to help many kinds of students.
- The instructor is sensitive to individual interests and abilities.

Clarity

- The instructor responds to questions clearly.
- The instructor emphasizes major points in the delivery of the subject matter.
- The instructor explains the subject matter clearly.
- The instructor relates course material to practical situations.

Impact on learning

- The instructor helps develop rational thinking.
- The instructor helps develop problem-solving ability.
- The instructor helps develop skills/techniques/views needed in the field.
- The instructor broadens student views.
- The instructor encourages the development of students' analytic ability.
- The instructor provides a healthy challenge to former attitudes.
- The instructor helps develop students' creative capacity.
- The instructor fosters respect for diverse points of view.
- The instructor sensitizes students to views or feelings of others.
- The instructor helps develop students' decision-making abilities.
- The instructor develops students' appreciation of intellectual activity.
- The instructor develops students' cultural awareness.
- The instructor helps students develop awareness of the process used to gain new knowledge.
- The instructor stimulates independent thinking.

Overall

- The overall teaching performance of the instructor is high.

Chism, N.V.N. (2007). *Peer Review of Teaching: A Sourcebook*. Bolton, MA: Anker.

Teacher Behavior Systems

Systematic processes for coding teacher behaviors have been developed by several researchers. Among the most popular is the Flanders Interaction Analysis System. It focuses on teacher talk and student talk and includes a category for other behaviors. Many other systems are modifications of the Flanders System and include nonverbal behaviors as well. The systems are used to provide precise analysis of classrooms and are especially suitable for situations in which the amount or kind of teacher talk is the main interest.

In one system, called the Cognitive Interaction Analysis System (CIAS), after a period of observing the class without recording, the rater makes a category notation every three seconds about the nature of the interaction that has occurred during that time period. Categories and a sample completed rating form follow for the Cognitive Interaction Analysis System, described in Lewis (2001).

Expanded CIAS Categories

1. Accepting student attitudes
   - 1h   Use of humor
   - 1f   Affective instructor comments
2. Positive reinforcement
3. Repeating a student response.
   - 3f   Giving corrective feedback
   - 3b   Building on a student response
4. Asking questions
   - 4c   Knowledge/comprehension level
   - 4e   Application (example) level
   - 4a   Analysis level
   - 4y   Synthesis level
   - 4j   Evaluation (judgment) level
   - 4f   Affective questions
   - 4s   Process or structure questions
   - 4r   Rhetorical questions
   - 4p   Probing questions
5. Lecturing
   - 5v   Simultaneous visual and verbal presentation
   - 5e   Using examples/analogies
   - 5r   Reviewing
   - 5x   Answering a student question

Chism, N.V.N. (2007). *Peer Review of Teaching: A Sourcebook.* Bolton, MA: Anker.

5m Mumbling
5t Reading verbatim from text/overhead/board/slide
6. Providing cues
6m Focusing on main points
6d Giving directions
6c Calling on a student
6s Giving assignments/process
6v Cues with visual presentation
7. Criticism of student answer/behavior
8. Cognitive student talk
8c–8j Answers to teacher questions
8n Student doesn't know answer
8q Student question
8h Student laughter
8g Students working in groups
8i Students working individually
9. Noncognitive student talk
10. Silence
0b Writing on board/overhead without talking
0m Mumbling (a general low roar)
0l Listening/watching

Chism, N.V.N. (2007). *Peer Review of Teaching: A Sourcebook*. Bolton, MA: Anker.

Some Typical CIAS Category Sequences and Their Explanations

Each sequence of CIAS codes is read from the top of the column to the bottom. The comment section interprets the interaction pattern which is represented by the codes to the left of it.

Sequence	Comment
6s 6s 6d 6d 6 6c 8q	This sequence indicates that the instructor began by giving the students an assignment (6s) or indicated a procedure for them to follow in completing an assignment. Directions for completing this process were then given (6d). The instructor then told the students what they were going to be covering that day in the lecture (6). This is followed by the instructor calling on a student (6c) who then asks a question (8q).
4a 4a 0 0 8a 8q 8q 5x 5x	In this sequence, the instructor asks a question that would be classified as being at the analysis level (4a). The question is then followed by six seconds of silence, or "think time" (0), and finally, the question is answered by a student (8a). When the students ask a question, it is recorded as 8q. The instructor's answer to that question is recorded as 5x. This provides information as to whether the instructor is spending adequate time or too much time in answering each student's question.
4e 4e 8e 8e 8e 2 3 3b	This sequence shows that the instructor asked a question at the application level (4e), and it was answered by a student (8e). It took the student 9 seconds to answer the question. This is typical for a higher level question. The instructor then praised the student's answer (i.e., "That's right, Joe."), repeated the student's answer so the rest of the class could hear it, and then used the student's answer to explain the concept further (3b).

Chism, N.V.N. (2007). *Peer Review of Teaching: A Sourcebook*. Bolton, MA: Anker.

Chapter 7

Peer Review in Special Contexts

Although most college and university teaching occurs in the fairly traditional format of classroom meetings, several disciplines employ instructional approaches that require additional discussion of peer review strategies. These include those disciplines that use performance-based instruction, where apprentices work onsite or in simulated laboratory, studio, clinic, or other practice settings, such as public school classrooms or social work clinics. The increasing use of technology in courses delivered wholly or in part over the World Wide Web creates other venues for peer review of teaching. Finally, special format teaching, such as service-learning and problem-based learning or case study approaches, as well as team teaching in any setting, requires some unique attention during the peer review process. This chapter will outline specific considerations for these settings.

Laboratories

In the laboratory, instructors' roles can vary widely. While the basic tasks are to design the activities, ensure that appropriate materials and conditions are provided, enforce safety procedures, coach student performance, and assess results, some instructors might also oversee the work of laboratory assistants, an additional dimension of work for peer review consideration. For large introductory courses, the instructor's role in the laboratory might be that of a "CEO" who interacts occasionally with laboratory teachers and students. On the opposite end of the spectrum, an instructor might be responsible for designing and implementing all aspects of a laboratory course. Both classroom observation and review of materials are the main methods for gathering data on these activities, but special items connected with the specific setting will help to focus review of these activities. A form for this purpose is contained in the resource materials section of this chapter, although a more general form may be used with particular items about laboratory instruction added, such as those in the resource materials section for Chapter 6. An additional form that might be mined for applicable items to the supervision of graduate student teaching assistants or graduate students doing research in laboratories is contained in the resource materials section of Chapter 8.

Studios

Studios where creative activity is situated, such as fine arts, music, theater, and architecture classrooms, are somewhat similar to laboratory settings with respect to the main tasks that instructors are expected to perform: designing activities, ensuring that appropriate materials and conditions are provided, and coaching and assessing performance. Here the difference from traditional settings is often in the type of design, coaching, and assessment activities. The instructional design may often be more open-ended than in laboratory situations and the coaching and assessment associated more with a connoisseurship model (Eisner, 2001) than a convergent match of results to expectations. The form in the resource materials section of this chapter reflects adaptation of standard observation and materials review forms for these settings.

Practice Settings

In professional fields such as the health sciences, education, and social work, much of the instruction takes place off campus in the actual settings where professionals in the field work. Often, students are supervised by preceptors, master teachers, and working professionals in the field. Peer review of these faculty is an integral part of the campus plan if they are, like clinical faculty, considered faculty and thus take part in the overall faculty evaluation system, but it might also be beneficial in informally determining which onsite supervisors are the most desirable for future placements and in coaching these instructors to be more helpful in promoting student learning. The main campus instructor can also be the subject of peer review focused on the way in which he or she designs these experiences, works with the onsite supervisors, and communicates with students. An example of a form that is used by the Indiana University School of Social Work for review of faculty liaisons to field instructors is included in the resource materials section of this chapter.

In addition to routine formal arrangements for student placements in practica associated with professional fields, special aspects of more traditional courses might also include onsite components for students. An example is service-learning. Here, the performance of both main instructor and site mentor can be assessed through peer review. Since service-learning often constitutes a component of a course rather than the entire course, it may be necessary to combine several instruments to arrive at an appropriate approach to peer review in these circumstances, or to add questions about these specific approaches to a more general instrument. Principles of good practice, such as those written by Howard (2001) for the University of Michigan, might be used as the basis for the service-learning component of the forms. Ideas for items that might be asked are found on a form in the resource materials section of this chapter.

THE SPECIAL CASE OF CLINICAL TEACHING IN THE HEALTH SCIENCES

Professionals in the health science education fields have done considerable work in devising systems of peer review of teaching. Lecture-based instruction (often called "didactic instruction") in such fields as medicine, dentistry, and nursing can be assessed in similar fashion to other traditional settings, yet instruction that takes place in health care settings through grand rounds, supervision of internships, and demonstration and performance coaching requires additional discussion.

Ludwick, Dieckman, Herdtner, Dugan, and Roche (1998) described clinical teaching as more unpredictable, emotional, and less static than teaching in a traditional classroom or science laboratory, emphasizing that all clinics exist to provide patient care and that providing care without compromising patient safety is the first priority. A panel of the Association of American Medical Colleges (Nutter et al., 2000) produced a comprehensive list of activities of medical school faculty in education. The clinical activity list included performing inpatient teaching during attending rounds, teaching during inpatient consultation rounds, teaching in surgery or special clinical procedure rooms, serving as preceptor for student-house staff patient care teams, serving as outpatient attending, serving as ambulatory care preceptor, serving as case-based session leader in wards or in clinic, serving as clinical conference leader, conducting student or resident morning report, and serving as house staff. The diversity of activities as well as multiple venues and times when teaching occurs provides a challenge for developing a peer review system. Additionally, the extent to which peer review takes time from revenue-generating activities is of concern in medical settings and will impact how much peer review is done and who will do it.

Much of the literature on evaluation of clinical teaching focuses on development and validation of instruments administered to medical students and residents. Many of these have their roots in the Stanford Faculty Development Program (SFDP) instrument (cited in Speer & Elnicki, 1999). This 26-item questionnaire includes items for seven categories: learning climate, control of session, communication of goals, understanding and retention, evaluation, feedback, and self-directed learning. The Mayo Teaching Evaluation Form (Beckman et al., 2003) added 16 items to 12 items from the Stanford questionnaire. The University of Michigan Global Rating Scale, a single item, 5-point global measure, produced similar results to the SFDP questionnaire when administered to senior medical residents (Williams, Litzelman, Babbott, Lubitz, & Hofer, 2002). The reliability of published clinical teaching review instruments has been reviewed by Beckman, Ghosh, Cook, Erwin, and Mandrekar (2004). Using qualitative analysis of interviews with residents, Bellman (2004) produced a list of 25 items related to good clinical teaching. Comparing the results from three peer evaluators, Beckman, Lee, Rohren, and Pankratz (2003) found the most reliable items were from the Control of Session, Evaluation, and Self-directed Learning categories, and the least from Communication of Goals. Ratings produced by resident and peer physicians were compared, and the peer physicians provided lower ratings that had higher inter-rater and internal reliabilities. In arguing for the advantages of peer review of teaching, Beckman (2004) provides a personal perspective on the benefits of the time spent in peer observation.

The items in the major instruments for residents to evaluate teaching in clinical settings have been adapted for the purpose of peer review by several institutions. Examples include those developed at:

- University of Washington School of Dentistry
  www.dental.washington.edu/aptmanual/appendix3.htm
- University of Texas Dental Branch at Houston
  www.db.uth.tmc.edu/prof-develop/Prof-Devdocs/PeerReviewPlanof
  Teaching2.htm#Unstructured_Clinical
- University of Medicine and Dentistry of New Jersey
  http://cte.umdnj.educareer_development/career_peer_review.cfm
- Kent State University College of Nursing
  www.kent.edu/nursing/Facultyupload/Teaching-Evaluation-Form-2.doc

A form that exemplifies elements of common peer review of clinical teaching instruments can be found in the resource materials section of this chapter.

While most of the attention in the literature on clinical teaching is devoted to validation of instrumentation, it should be stressed that an overall approach to peer review must be more comprehensive. Since there are usually limited teaching materials produced by the clinical teacher, observation of clinical teaching will be the mainstay of peer review, yet a peer review of teaching plan needs to do more than provide validated rating forms for this observation. Ways to understand the teaching philosophy of the clinical instructor—the thinking behind the teaching—should be part of the process. Reflective notes or notes from a pre- or post-observation discussion constitute additional data that might be collected. These methods should be included in a plan that specifies who will be reviewed, by whom, when, and for what purposes, as described in Chapter 2.

Problem-Based Learning or Case Study Learning

Problem-based learning (PBL), or other approaches in which the instructor takes on a tutorial or facilitator approach, will look different than the traditional classroom, yet can benefit from peer review of teaching. In some PBL settings, in fact, the word *instructor* is avoided in favor of *tutor* or *facilitator* to convey the indirect role that he or she is to take. Often, PBL and case study approaches are associated with the health sciences, engineering, business, or other professional fields, but PBL, simulations, and cases can be a component of instruction in any field. In these forms of instruction, the instructor's role is to facilitate exploration of specific problems or cases. He or she fosters the process of learning, modeling what students should do to engage a problem and access the information they need to address it. The goal is for students to become master learners. Frequently, the cases or problems that are used to stimulate the learning experiences are not prepared by the instructor, and in such instances, it will be important for the reviewer to separate out observations directly tied to the content of the material and its design from observations about the instructor. In cases where the instructor has authored the materials, the review can encompass the materials as well.

The main emphasis in PBL and tutorial learning is the instructor as learning coach. Prompted by the case or simulation, the student is to do the major work of analyzing the situation and deciding what needs to be learned in order to do so. In some variations of PBL, the steps to be followed by the tutor are quite clearly delineated. Instructors are given clear guides to action and the role is highly prescribed. Peer review thus has to take these into account, yet there are still characteristics of the instructor's approach, such as their listening skills, content knowledge, and interpersonal rapport, that render some instructors more effective in these coaching situations than others. A general form that focuses on such considerations is included in the resource materials section of this chapter. A sample form from the Indiana University School of Dentistry is also provided.

Team Teaching

The popularity of learning communities and other approaches that call for multiple instructors to work together in the design and delivery of instruction, often in cross-disciplinary contexts, requires additional adaptation for peer review of teaching approaches. As with student ratings of teaching in these settings, it is important, but difficult, to separate out the contributions of each faculty member for analysis. Since these are blended into the gestalt of the class, but also conditioned by each other, it is impossible to treat them completely separately. Nevertheless, the attempt to do so must be made within the context of evaluation of teaching systems that focus on individual performance, which is the most common context for appraisal. Students are often asked to complete separate ratings of each instructor in a team-taught situation, but this solution is usually unsatisfactory in that it does not acknowledge the interaction effects. Items that are more specific to the team teaching context are included in the resource materials section of this chapter for use in these settings. They focus on both observation and materials, but include some exploration of the instructor's stated approach and analysis of the respective contributions and impact of other team members.

Online Teaching

Increasingly, the use of information technologies is a part of course design. Most courses now use a course management system such as Blackboard, Angel, or an institution-specific program to store the syllabus, calendar, handouts, and other instructional materials of the course. Some use these systems to conduct online discussions, perform assessments, or host group projects. While most of these courses also maintain an in-person component, some are conducted entirely in a virtual environment.

One effect of this use of information technology is that, to the extent to which peers may access these course environments, it is more open to review. As Bass (2000) points out, "In order to evaluate something, you have to be able to see it, and there is perhaps no greater impact of the new technologies on the educational environment than their capacity to make both learning and reflective teaching visible" (p. 38). Lee Shulman's (1993) call for teaching as community property is being heeded. Reviewers now have a window into teaching previously not as completely available because they can now listen to the dialogue between teacher and students, witness the ways in which course goals and materials are presented, and observe how the learning is assessed and feedback is provided. The routine archiving of these course records over time also presents the opportunity to take a longitudinal look at the teaching of any one instructor.

Depending on the extent to which technology is used in any course, there are a number of elements that can serve as the basis for peer review. In a course where only the syllabus is online, there would be no advantage to reviewing the electronic over the paper form, unless there are live links or other features that make it different. However, when the instructor conducts a weekly online discussion that is stored within the course management environment, a classroom record that would be hard to capture in such detail through an instance of classroom observation in a face-to-face class is available for the analysis of a peer. Furthermore, capturing these data means that distance no longer limits the potential pool of peers since peers at other institutions are able to review the student–faculty interactions in the course without visiting a classroom on another campus.

Much has been written about the evaluation of online courses, primarily about student rating of instruction for such courses, but there is also a substantial body of literature in the instructional design literature on technical considerations, which are an additional dimension of these courses. Many of the other components of the assessment of online courses are similar to those that one would apply to in-person courses or course materials. In the instruments that are part of the resource materials section of this chapter, the components are usually broken down into separate sections. The examples are taken from the criteria in use for courses developed through the Indiana University School of Nursing and the JumpStart program of the Center for Teaching and Learning at the Office for Professional Development at Indiana University–Purdue University Indianapolis (IUPUI). Note that Section C of the latter instrument references the institutional learning goals at IUPUI and thus ties the review of the course to campus goals. Even though these goals will be different for users from other institutions, this part of the form is included to show how alignment with institutional principles can be built into an instrument.

In addition to reviewing the course as a course, peer review of online instruction may involve technology and accessibility considerations as well. If the instructor is not responsible for these components, it would be inappropriate to review them, but when the instructor is integrally involved in the technology issues, forms similar to additional ones in use at IUPUI may be considered part of the peer review. Forms that speak to technology standards and accessibility considerations are included in the resource materials section of this chapter.

Situating the review of an online course within an overall plan for peer review of teaching is an important task addressed by Cobb, Billings, Mays, and Canty-Mitchell (2001). The authors discuss establishing norms and values for the review, criteria for judging the course, procedures for conducting the review, selection of peer reviewers, and follow-up activities. The form they developed for the Indiana University School of Nursing, available in the resource materials section of this chapter, is based on the Seven Principles for Good Practice in Undergraduate Education (Chickering & Gamson, 1987). Although they do not include specific design considerations on their form, they enumerate the following in their text: provision of orientation to software, inviting and consistent web design, ways to bookmark and access resources, easy-to-use navigation tools, clear and functional graphics, fast download time, and readability.

Bass (2000) offers some additional insights into the evaluation of teaching in technology environments, recommending:

- Situating the evaluation within a context of innovation and inquiry—stress scholarship and reflection on the part of the teacher
- Including flexibility in the design of the evaluation—be sure that instruments and methods can adapt to changing conditions as technology and intended outcomes change
- Distinguishing between workload and intellectual work—the labor intensity of course production activity should not take priority over the thoughtfulness involved
- Seeing the teaching in a communal context—often a team of people have produced the course and the course itself is part of a broader educational endeavor
- Recognizing the double bind of faculty who work in these environments—they are doing different work, but judged by standards of equivalence to traditional approaches.

The Special Case of Online Repositories

A form of peer review of instructional materials that has emerged in the past decade is peer review for inclusion in online teaching repositories. These collections of electronic materials make specific methodological suggestions, handouts, content modules, exercises, assessment strategies, and other instructional materials available to instructors who might want to use them. Some repositories are multidisciplinary and others are discipline-specific. Most make the materials openly available free of charge, although some carry charges or restrict access. Not all are peer reviewed, but those that are have developed processes and instruments that reviewers use.

This form of peer review can be embedded in institutional peer review. For example, having an instructional module accepted into a repository would likely be considered a form of "publication" and because it has been externally judged as valuable, might add to the ability of a faculty member in making his or her case for promotion and tenure. Bass (2000) points out that such public review situates the teaching within the context of scholarly inquiry.

Two examples of peer-reviewed repositories will be described here: MERLOT (www .merlot.org) and the MedEdPORTAL of the Association of American Medical Colleges (www.aamc.org/mededportal).

MERLOT (Multimedia Educational Resource for Learning and Online Teaching) was established in 1997 and resides at the California State Center for Distributed Learning. With a network of partnerships to sustain it, MERLOT is a collection of online materials organized by discipline and available to users without charge as well as a community of scholars who hold meetings and collaborate to improve the MERLOT resource and higher education generally. A major goal "is to improve the effectiveness of teaching and learning by increasing the quantity and quality of peer reviewed online learning materials that can be easily incorporated into faculty designed courses" (MERLOT, 2006a).

The peer review process used by MERLOT has a special purpose:

> The primary purpose of these reviews is to allow faculty from any institution of higher education to decide if the online teaching-learning materials they are examining will work in their course(s). The emphasis on the user's perspective is the reason peer reviews are performed by peer users of instructional technology, and not necessarily peer authors of instructional technology. (MERLOT, 2006b)

Submissions to MERLOT are first screened by an editorial board for the related disciplinary area of the submission. If a submission is determined to be of high quality, it is passed along to two higher education faculty members who do a "composite review" that is posted publicly with the material. The review form used by reviewers is included in the resource materials section of this chapter.

Interestingly, MERLOT also exemplifies, through its "star" system, formative peer review of teaching. Items are rated with as many as five stars, with five being the highest sign of quality. Items that receive fewer than three stars are still made available in the hopes that browsers of the repository will glean some ideas from even an incompletely realized resource, or that the author will take the advice of the reviewers and further develop the resource and resubmit the improved version. The web site advises:

> MERLOT is a resource of End Products and Developing Products. The End Products should be ready for immediate and effective use. Developing Prod-

ucts are at an early or intermediate stage of development and will by definition have problems. Both End Products and Developing Products provide ideas and guidelines for developers and users of instructional technology. It will be critical to support the Developing Products because we need to create a process for encouraging the expansion of the collection. (MERLOT, 2006c)

MedEdPORTAL (Providing Online Resources to Advance Learning) is a collection of peer-reviewed instructional materials for medical education, overseen by an editorial board and a group of content editors with specific areas of expertise, such as assessment or virtual patient approaches. They assign each submission to three reviewers who are faculty or graduate trained educators at medical schools. Their criteria are illustrated in the form in the resource materials section of this chapter.

Although many of the more common contexts have been discussed in this chapter, it is by no means exhaustive of the special contexts and approaches that may be the focus of peer review of teaching. Modifications of existing resources may be needed in the development of special instruments to assist with peer review in these situations. Another approach is to start with a list of the desired characteristics of teaching in the special setting or context, given the learning goals, and to create an entirely new guide to peer review in these situations.

Resource Materials

Peer Review in Special Contexts

Peer Review of Laboratory Instruction

Peer Review of Studio Instruction

Peer Review of Teaching in Non-Medical Field Settings

Excerpts From a Form for Field Instructor Evaluation of the Field Liaison Instructor, Indiana University School of Social Work

Peer Review of Clinical Teaching

Peer Review of Teaching in Service-Learning or Civic Engagement Contexts

Peer Review of Team Teaching

Peer Review of Instruction in Problem-Based Learning or Case Study Settings

Dimensions of Tutor Performance Assessed in Problem-Based Learning Settings at the Indiana University School of Dentistry

Peer Review of Web-Based Instruction

Sample Form for Evaluating Online Courses From Indiana University–Purdue University Indianapolis

Technical Guidelines for IUPUI JumpStart Course Development

Peer Review Form for MERLOT

MedEdPORTAL Digital and Educational Peer Review Form

Peer Review of Laboratory Instruction

These items were developed with science labs in mind, but might also apply to computer labs or hands-on experiences in various disciplines. The items are based on having access to instructional materials as well as to direct observation. As with other forms of review, they assume that some way of understanding the thinking behind the instructor's approach, such as a conversation or reading of self-reflections, has also been a part of the review. For formative peer review, the questions might be used to collect data for a feedback session or coaching document. For summative purposes, a rating form can be composed of relevant items, or a narrative summary prepared speaking to the relevant items, comparing the instructor to peers.

Design of Learning Experiences

- Are learning experiences relevant to the course curriculum?
- Do they reflect current practice in the field?
- Are they at an appropriate level of challenge for students?
- Are the goals clear?
- Is the assessment strategy appropriate to the goals?

Instructions or Procedures Materials

- Are instructions and procedures clear?
- Are they of appropriate length for the time allocated?
- Do they contain information on goals and assessment?
- Are they proofread and in a readable format?
- Are the materials needed for the laboratory available?

Instructional Oversight

- Does the laboratory instructor show understanding of the goals and procedures?
- Does he or she demonstrate the relevant content knowledge needed for the laboratory session(s)?
- Does the instructor take a proactive role in engaging with the students in the lab?
- Is the instructor available for questions and assistance?
- In helping students, does the instructor use clear questioning and coaching strategies?
- Can the instructor use the equipment and demonstrate the techniques needed for the laboratory?
- Are safety procedures followed?
- Does the instructor coordinate work with any laboratory assistants, if present?

Chism, N.V.N. (2007). *Peer Review of Teaching: A Sourcebook.* Bolton, MA: Anker.

Student Engagement

- Are students actively engaged in following the procedures?
- Do students show understanding of lab goals and procedures?
- As they have questions, do students ask the instructor for help?
- If students are working in groups, do they work well as teams?
- Do students reach results that appear to satisfy them?

Assessment

- Is the assessment procedure at an appropriate level of challenge?
- Are assessment procedures clear to the students?
- Does student work show evidence of achieving the goals?
- Do instructor comments on graded work provide ample and helpful feedback?

Comments on overall performance of instructor:

Chism, N.V.N. (2007). *Peer Review of Teaching: A Sourcebook.* Bolton, MA: Anker.

Peer Review of Studio Instruction

These items were developed for use primarily in the visual arts, music, drama, architecture, or related fields. The items are based on having access to instructional materials as well as to direct observation. As with other forms of review, they assume that some way of understanding the thinking behind the instructor's approach, such as a conversation or reading of self-reflections, has also been a part of the review. For formative peer review, the questions might be used to collect data for a feedback session or coaching document. For summative purposes, a rating form can be composed of relevant items, or a narrative summary prepared speaking to the relevant items, comparing the instructor to peers.

Design of Learning Experiences

- Are the learning experiences relevant to the course curriculum?
- Are the goals in line with current exemplary practice in the field (methods of dramatic coaching, architectural review, visual arts instruction, etc.)
  Here, specific items relating to the values and standards of the field would be inserted to trigger the review of specific elements.
- Are the learning experiences at an appropriate level of challenge for the students?
- Are the goals clear?
- Is the assessment strategy appropriate to the goals?

Instructions or Procedures Materials

- Are instructions and procedures clear?
- Are they of appropriate length for the time allocated?
- Do they contain information on goals and assessment?
- If printed, are they proofread and in a readable format?
- Are the materials needed for the experience available?

Instructional Oversight

- Does the studio instructor show understanding of the goals and procedures?
- Does he or she demonstrate the relevant content knowledge needed for the session(s)?
- Does the instructor proactively engage with the students?
- Is the instructor available for questions and assistance?
- In helping students, does the instructor use clear questioning and coaching strategies?
- Can the instructor demonstrate the techniques needed for the session?
- Are safety procedures followed (if applicable)?
- Does the instructor coordinate work with any instructional assistants, if present?

Chism, N.V.N. (2007). *Peer Review of Teaching: A Sourcebook.* Bolton, MA: Anker.

Student Engagement
- Are students actively engaged in following the procedures?
- Do students show understanding of the studio goals and procedures?
- As they have questions, do students ask the instructor for help?
- If students are working in groups, do they work well as teams?
- Do students reach results that appear to satisfy them?

Assessment
- Is the assessment procedure at an appropriate level of challenge?
- Are assessment procedures clear to students?
- Does the instructor use a rubric or other vehicle to link specific grades with performance expectations?
- Does student work show evidence of achieving the goals?
- Do instructor comments, both in the studio and on any written feedback forms that might be used, provide ample and helpful feedback?

Other comments:

Chism, N.V.N. (2007). *Peer Review of Teaching: A Sourcebook*. Bolton, MA: Anker.

Peer Review of Teaching in Non-Medical Field Settings

These items were developed with settings such as P–12 classrooms, corporate environments, or social service agencies in mind. They are based on having access to instructional materials as well as to direct observation. As with other forms of review, they assume that some way of understanding the thinking behind the instructor's approach, such as a conversation or reading of self-reflections, has also been a part of the review. For formative peer review, the questions might be used to collect data for a feedback session or coaching document. For summative purposes, a rating form can be composed of relevant items, or a narrative summary prepared speaking to the relevant items, comparing the instructor to peers.

Design of Learning Experience

- Is the experience relevant to the course curriculum?
- Are the goals in line with current exemplary practice in the field (reflective practice, evidence-based decision-making, etc.)
  Here, specific items relating to the values and standards of the field would be inserted to trigger the review of specific elements.
- Is the choice of setting appropriate for the learning goals?
- Are the goals clear?
- Is the assessment strategy appropriate to the goals?

Instructional Oversight *(assumption is that there is a field supervisor and a college/university instructor)*

College/University Instructor

- Is the instructor onsite an appropriate amount of time?
- While onsite, does the instructor collaborate well with the field-based supervisor?

If the instructor is involved in direct supervision, the questions in the next section might also apply to him or her. Also see the next form, which focuses exclusively on this role.

Field-Based Supervisor

- Does the field instructor show understanding of the goals and procedures?
- Does he or she select appropriate learning experiences for students?
- Does he or she demonstrate the relevant content knowledge needed to assist the students?
- Does the instructor demonstrate good understanding and model use of exemplary practice in the setting?

Chism, N.V.N. (2007*). Peer Review of Teaching: A Source*book. Bolton, MA: Anker.

- Is the instructor available for questions and assistance?
- In helping students, does the instructor use clear questioning and coaching strategies?

Student Engagement
- Are students actively engaged in the practice setting?
- Do students show understanding of the goals and procedures of their experience?
- As students have questions, do they ask the supervisor for help?
- If students are working in groups, do they work well as teams?

Assessment
- Is the assessment procedure at an appropriate level of challenge?
- Are assessment procedures clear to students?
- Is ongoing feedback as well as later reflection used to promote learning?
- Does student performance show evidence of achieving the goals?
- Do instructor comments on any written assessments provide ample and helpful feedback?

Other comments:

Chism, N.V.N. (2007). *Peer Review of Teaching: A Sourcebook*. Bolton, MA: Anker.

Excerpts From a Form for Field Instructor Evaluation of the Field Liaison Instructor, Indiana University School of Social Work

The purpose of this evaluation is to provide feedback to school administration and faculty concerning the nature and quality of field liaison activities. Because field liaison responsibilities are valued so highly, evaluations of the nature and quality of field liaison activities are considered along with other assessment data for purposes of promotion, tenure, salary increments, and other awards.

True-False

1. T   F   The faculty field liaison communicated with me early during the semester/year.
2. T   F   The field liaison visited with me at the agency during the semester/year.
3. T   F   The field liaison met with practicum student(s) during the semester/year.

> SA = Strongly agree
> A = Agree
> U = Undecided
> D = Disagree
> SD = Strongly disagree

4. The field liaison provided useful consultation about the school's curriculum.
5. The field liaison facilitated discussion of field practicum learning objectives.
6. The field liaison was helpful in reviewing students' written learning plans.
7. The field liaison helped to advance the quality of the field practicum experience.
8. The field liaison responded promptly to my needs as a field instructor.
9. The field liaison responded promptly to the needs of the practicum student(s).
10. The field liaison communicated with me at appropriate intervals.
11. The field liaison promptly responded to my calls and messages.
12. The field liaison addressed problems or issues that arose during the semester/year.
13. The field liaison expressed interest in the quality of students' learning.
14. The field liaison reviewed students' practicum assignments.
15. The field liaison helped to evaluate students' practicum performance.
16. The field liaison contributed significantly to the field practicum experience.
17. I would highly recommend this faculty field liaison to other field instructors.

Reprinted with permission.

Chism, N.V.N. (2007). *Peer Review of Teaching: A Sourcebook*. Bolton, MA: Anker.

Peer Review of Clinical Teaching

5 = Strongly agree
4 = Agree
3 = Neither agree nor disagree
2 = Disagree
1 = Strongly disagree

Professionalism

Demonstrates respect for patients, coworkers, and students	5	4	3	2	1
Demonstrates ethical conduct and discusses ethical issues with students	5	4	3	2	1
Exemplifies professionalism	5	4	3	2	1
Demonstrates enthusiasm	5	4	3	2	1
Serves as an appropriate clinical role model	5	4	3	2	1

Comments:

Technical Competence

Demonstrates up-to-date clinical skills	5	4	3	2	1
Demonstrates up-to-date knowledge	5	4	3	2	1
Develops an appropriate treatment plan	5	4	3	2	1

Comments:

Interaction With Students

Establishes rapport	5	4	3	2	1
Encourages all students to participate	5	4	3	2	1
Asks appropriate questions	5	4	3	2	1
Encourages students to defend their opinions	5	4	3	2	1
Elicits opinions before offering a diagnosis	5	4	3	2	1
Provides appropriate feedback	5	4	3	2	1

Comments:

Chism, N.V.N. (2007). *Peer Review of Teaching: A Sourcebook.* Bolton, MA: Anker.

Organization

Makes objectives and expectations clear	5	4	3	2	1
Uses time effectively	5	4	3	2	1

Comments:

Overall Evaluation

Exemplary   Excellent   Good   Fair   Poor

Additional comments:

Chism, N.V.N. (2007). *Peer Review of Teaching: A Sourcebook.* Bolton, MA: Anker.

Peer Review of Teaching in Service-Learning or Civic Engagement Contexts

The assumption in developing these items is that service-learning and civic engagement might be experiences nested within a more traditional course, or may be stand-alone experiences. The items are based on having access to instructional materials as well as to direct observation. As with other forms of review, they assume that some way of understanding the thinking behind the instructor's approach, such as a conversation or reading of self-reflections, has also been a part of the review. For formative peer review, the questions might be used to collect data for a feedback session or coaching document. For summative purposes, a rating form can be composed of relevant items, or a narrative summary prepared speaking to the relevant items, comparing the instructor to peers.

Design of Learning Experience

- Is the experience relevant to the course curriculum?
- Are the goals clear?
- Do the goals show concern for the blend of service and learning that is the desired outcome?
- Is the choice of setting appropriate for the learning goals?
- Is the service involved of benefit to the community?
- Is the assessment strategy appropriate to the goals?

Instructional Oversight *(only applicable in cases when the college/university instructor is onsite as well as a field supervisor)*

College/University Instructor

- Is the instructor onsite an appropriate amount of time?
- While onsite, does the instructor collaborate well with the field-based supervisor?

If the instructor is involved in direct supervision, the questions in the next section might also apply to him or her.

Field-Based Supervisor

- Does the field instructor show understanding of the goals and procedures?
- Does he or she provide appropriate learning experiences for students, given the course goals?
- Does he or she demonstrate the relevant content knowledge needed to assist the students?

Chism, N.V.N. (2007). *Peer Review of Teaching: A Sourcebook.* Bolton, MA: Anker.

- Does the instructor demonstrate good understanding and model use of exemplary practice in the setting?
- Is the instructor available for questions and assistance?
- In helping students, does the instructor use clear questioning and coaching strategies?

Student Engagement
- Are students actively engaged in the practice setting?
- Do students show understanding of the goals and procedures of their experience?
- As students have questions, do they ask the supervisor for help?
- If students are working in groups, do they work well as teams?

Assessment
- Is the assessment procedure at an appropriate level of challenge?
- Are assessment procedures clear to students?
- Is ongoing feedback as well as later reflection used to promote learning?
- Does student performance show evidence of achieving both course goals and benefit to the community?
- Do students develop civic awareness?
- Do instructor comments on any written assessments provide ample and helpful feedback?
- Do the assessments call for student reflection, input from the site partner, rubrics, or other ways of articulating the grading scheme?

Other comments:

Chism, N.V.N. (2007). *Peer Review of Teaching: A Sourcebook*. Bolton, MA: Anker.

Peer Review of Team Teaching

The term team teaching *can encompass a range of activities from extensive collaboration in planning and delivering an entire course to merely co-facilitating one module or learning experience. It is thus appropriate to assess the performance of each individual involved according to the procedures that have been developed for the kind of activity in which they have been active, such as instructional design, supervision of the laboratory, or the like. Comments on these forms might note the ways in which the team arrangement either facilitated or limited the performance of the individual. In addition, the items below can be addressed to assess how the person functioned as part of a team and how the team as a whole performed.*

The items are based on having access to instructional materials as well as to direct observation. As with other forms of review, they assume that some way of understanding the thinking behind the instructor's approach, such as a conversation or reading of self-reflections, has also been a part of the review. For formative peer review, the questions might be used to collect data for a feedback session or coaching document. For summative purposes, a rating form can be composed of relevant items, or a narrative summary prepared speaking to the relevant items, comparing the instructor to peers.

In looking at the instructional materials prepared by the team and discussing these with the instructor/team members or reading reflections about the instructor's involvement:

If the team member was to have been involved in course design
- Is there evidence that the instructor contributed positively to the design of the course by attending meetings and completing assignments?
- Did the instructor provide specific content knowledge and/or skills that were essential to the course?
- Did the instructor interact constructively with other members of the team?

If the team member was to have been involved in delivering the course
- Did the instructor contribute positively to the facilitation of learning in the setting?
- Did the instructor respect the presence of other team members and share the responsibilities appropriately to the agreed-upon design?
- Did the instructor integrate his or her perspective with that of other team members?

Chism, N.V.N. (2007). *Peer Review of Teaching: A Sourcebook.* Bolton, MA: Anker.

If the team member was involved in assessment
- Did the instructor adhere to the team's criteria and procedures for grading student work?
- Was the instructor prompt in returning assessments?
- Was the instructor available for coordinating discussions with team members concerning feedback and grading?

Overall
- Was the instructor helpful in advancing the thinking of team members?
- Did the instructor share authority and engage in collaborative decision-making well?
- Was the instructor responsible in attending meetings and contributing as planned?

Chism, N.V.N. (2007). *Peer Review of Teaching: A Sourcebook.* Bolton, MA: Anker.

Peer Review of Instruction in Problem-Based Learning or Case Study Settings

The items are based on having access to instructional materials as well as to direct observation. As with other forms of review, they assume that some way of understanding the thinking behind the instructor's approach, such as a conversation or reading of self-reflections, has also been a part of the review. For formative peer review, the questions might be used to collect data for a feedback session or coaching document. For summative purposes, a rating form can be composed of relevant items, or a narrative summary prepared speaking to the relevant items, comparing the instructor to peers.

Design of Learning Experiences *(to be used in reviews of the designer)*
- Are the cases or problems relevant to the course curriculum?
- Is the case or problem-based approach a desirable way to address course goals for this lesson or lessons?
- Do the cases or problems reflect current issues in the field?
- Is the planned student performance assessment strategy appropriate to the goals?

Instructions or Procedures Materials *(to be used in reviews of those who created these)*
- Are the cases or problems at an appropriate level of challenge for students?
- Do the cases or problems reflect important judgment issues or areas of content knowledge in the field?
- Are instructions and procedures clear?
- Are the cases or problems of appropriate length for the time allocated?
- Do they contain information on goals and assessment?
- Are they proofread and in a readable format?
- Are the materials needed for the analysis of the cases or problems available?

Instructional Oversight
- Does the instructor show understanding of the goals and procedures?
- Does he or she help students understand the relevant content knowledge needed for the cases or problems?
- Is the instructor available for assistance outside of class?
- In helping students, does the instructor use clear questioning strategies?
- Does the instructor show good listening skills?
- Does the instructor coach students to be reflective about their own learning?
- Does the instructor follow course procedures, if established, for working through each case or problem?
  If there are such procedures, such as refraining from giving answers or ensuring that each session is assessed, they may be itemized in separate goals in this section.

Chism, N.V.N. (2007). *Peer Review of Teaching: A Sourcebook.* Bolton, MA: Anker.

Student Engagement

- Are students actively engaged in addressing the cases or problems?
- Do they show understanding of the goals and procedures of the lessons?
- Do they interact with the instructor according to the ways that have been recommended by the approach?
- If students are working in groups, do they work well as teams?
- Do students follow up in independently researching information or doing other tasks connected with addressing the cases or problems?
- Do students reach results that appear to satisfy them?

Assessment

- Is the assessment procedure at an appropriate level of challenge?
- Are assessment procedures clear to students?
- Does student work show evidence of achieving the goals?
- Do instructor comments on graded work or verbal remarks provide ample and helpful feedback?

Other comments:

Chism, N.V.N. (2007). *Peer Review of Teaching: A Sourcebook*. Bolton, MA: Anker.

Dimensions of Tutor Performance Assessed in Problem-Based Learning Settings at the Indiana University School of Dentistry

Communication

- Modeled good listening skills and collegiality
- Utilized effective communication skills
- Encouraged the use of a variety of delivery methods and media
- Provided feedback about teaching methods utilized

Knowledge Base

- Facilitated the formulation of relevant and specific questions
- Facilitated the recognition of specific knowledge gaps
- Facilitated the generation of specific learning issues and hypotheses
- Facilitated the integration of the domains (biological, behavioral, population, and ethical)
- Facilitated the learning process without lecturing

Reasoning Process

- Encouraged the generation of learning issues that advanced the hypotheses
- Helped design strategies to obtain research and to resolve conflicting data
- Assisted in identifying appropriate resources and their critical review
- Promoted evidence-based learning
- Promoted the scientific process
- Encouraged clear and concise summaries

Professionalism

- Attended all tutorials and arrived punctually
- Modeled and promoted courteous, respectful, honest, and ethical behavior
- Facilitated the PBL process
- Promoted healthy group dynamics
- Exemplified professionalism in appearance, speech, and behavior

Assessment

- Modeled responsibility and self-awareness
- Facilitated assessments (self, peers, group, and tutor)
- Performed self-assessment and modeled how to use constructive criticism
- Aided in identifying strategies for improvement and assisted in their implementation

Reprinted with permission.

Chism, N.V.N. (2007). *Peer Review of Teaching: A Source*book. Bolton, MA: Anker.

Peer Review of Web-Based Instruction

Rate the following using a scale from 1 to 5 with 1 being the lowest and 5 being the highest score.

Course Materials

1. Goals or learning outcomes of the course are clearly stated.
2. Goals or learning outcomes are appropriate to the level of the learner.
3. Course guidelines provide a clear indication to students as to their responsibilities in the course.
4. Course guidelines provide a clear indication of how student progress will be evaluated (e.g., required papers, participation, discussion, or debate).
5. Course guidelines provide a clear indication of how the grades will be assigned (e.g., standards for papers, quizzes, discussion).

Principles of Good Practice

6. Students have an opportunity to interact with the faculty member (e.g., asynchronous, synchronous communication, private email, telephone, or fax).
7. Students have an opportunity to interact with each other (e.g., asynchronous, synchronous communication, private email, telephone, or fax).
8. Students are provided with prompt feedback on assignments.
9. Students are actively involved in the learning process.
10. Students spend a sufficient amount of time in the learning process.
11. The faculty member sets realistic, yet high expectations for all students in the teaching-learning process.
12. The faculty member respects diverse talents and ways of learning (e.g., a variety of learning experiences are assigned).
13. Students are expected to cooperate with one another on assigned tasks.

Graphic Design Principles

14. Web page design is inviting to look at and draws the students' attention.
15. There is evidence that the principle of proximity* is adhered to throughout the course.
16. There is evidence that the principle of contrast* is adhered to throughout the course.
17. There is evidence that the principle of alignment* is adhered to throughout the course.

Chism, N.V.N. (2007). *Peer Review of Teaching: A Sourcebook*. Bolton, MA: Anker.

18. There is evidence that the principle of repetition* is adhered to throughout the course.

19. Fonts are sans serif rather than serif.

Additional comments:

*Form provided in Cobb, Billings, Mays, and Canty-Mitchell (2001). Peer review of teaching in web-based courses in nursing. Nurse Educator, 26(6), 274–279. Reprinted with permission. The authors take these principles from Williams and Tollett (1998). Proximity refers to the relation of elements to each other, such as headlines to subheads to related text. Contrast is the use of visual elements such as color, font, and graphics to direct the eye. Alignment stresses lining up pages in similar manner. Repetition is the repeated use of elements that tie the course together such as navigation buttons.

Chism, N.V.N. (2007). Peer Review of Teaching: A Sourcebook. Bolton, MA: Anker.

Sample Form for Evaluating Online Courses
From Indiana University–Purdue University Indianapolis

Instructional Design and Development Guidelines for Teams Developing IUPUI JumpStart Courses	
Section A. General Guidelines	
Course learning objectives:	▪ are clearly stated ▪ are written from learner's point of view ▪ are appropriate for the target audience ▪ require that students spend a portion of the course engaging in higher levels of learning, such as analysis, synthesis, and evaluation ▪ are measurable ▪ are appropriately sequenced ▪ are congruent with activities and assessment strategies
Course activities:	▪ include clear instructions ▪ are appropriate for target audience ▪ are appropriate for desired skill level ▪ provide variety and use several different instructional methods ▪ are used to engage students in the learning process ▪ appropriately capitalize on the capabilities of the technology (e.g., use of discussion forums, guest lecturers, virtual tours, and other opportunities not available in the traditional site-based classroom) ▪ provide students with opportunities to apply course concepts to authentic situations ▪ offer students some opportunity for choice ▪ are congruent with objectives and assessment strategies
Course assessment strategies:	▪ include clear instructions ▪ are performed frequently ▪ are designed to gather both formative and summative information ▪ are appropriate for audience ▪ are appropriate for desired skill level ▪ clearly communicate expectations with respect to quality of work desired ▪ include multiple opportunities for feedback ▪ are congruent with objectives and activities ▪ are designed in such a way that when the electronic testing tool is used for formal "high-stakes" testing, methods are used to promote test integrity and security (e.g., randomized questions, randomized choices, changes in the test from semester to semester, etc.)
The course integrates good practice by:	▪ encouraging contact between faculty and students ▪ developing reciprocity and cooperation among students ▪ using active learning techniques ▪ giving prompt feedback ▪ emphasizing time on task ▪ communicating high expectations ▪ respecting diverse talents and ways of learning

continued on next page

Chism, N.V.N. (2007*). Peer Review of Teaching: A Sourceb*ook. Bolton, MA: Anker.

Instructional Design and Development Guidelines for Teams Developing IUPUI JumpStart Courses	
Section B: Team Guidelines for Developing a Complete Syllabus	
The syllabus is complete and provides information with respect to:	• course title • course number • course section • instructions regarding how to communicate with the instructor and other students (via phone, email, coursemail, etc.) • required textbooks, reading packets with detailed information and indication of availability • course description from university catalog • prerequisite courses • prerequisite content knowledge and technical skills • course goals and objectives • content outline and course calendar that includes schedule of assignments such as readings, exams, papers, and other requested learning assessment activities • grading standards and criteria • a statement that provides an estimate of the expected student workload • a statement that discusses specific expectations for students working in the online environment • a description of minimum hardware and software requirements • instructions for handling technical problems with the server, the ISP, the PC, and Oncourse • participation policy (includes information about participation in online group activities such as discussion forums, etc.) • instructions regarding submission of assignments (e.g., via drop box? attachment to email? postal service?) • approximate expected timelines for instructor responses to student messages • make-up or late assignment policy • text/exam policy • extra credit policy • extension policy • illness policy • cheating and plagiarism policy • special accommodations policy • P/F, I, and W grading policy • statement regarding civility • disclaimer regarding policies subject to change

continued on next page

Chism, N.V.N. (2007). *Peer Review of Teaching: A Sourcebook.* Bolton, MA: Anker.

Instructional Design and Development Guidelines for Teams Developing IUPUI JumpStart Courses	
The syllabus also contains the following recommended information, such as:	▪ a statement regarding beliefs about teaching and learning and the instructional methods used ▪ an explanation of the conceptual structure used to organize the course ▪ a bibliography of supplemental readings ▪ a list of campus resources for tutoring and academic support ▪ a list of cocurricular activities relevant to your course ▪ supplemental material to help students be successful in your course
The course includes links to appropriate support resources, such as:	▪ the UITS (computing support) Helpdesk ▪ the UITS (computing support) Knowledge Base ▪ tutoring centers (e.g., the writing center, the speech center, the math lab, etc.) ▪ professional organizations
Section C: Team Guidelines for Integrating IUPUI PULs Into JumpStart Courses	
The undergraduate course focuses on one or more of the following Principles of Undergraduate Learning:	1. **Core Communication and Quantitative Skills** (Definition: The ability of students to write, read, speak, and listen, perform quantitative analysis, and use information resources and technology—the foundation skills necessary for all IUPUI students to succeed.) Outcomes: This set of skills is demonstrated, respectively, by the ability to: a) express ideas and facts to others effectively in a variety of written formats b) comprehend, interpret, and analyze texts c) communicate orally in one-on-one and group settings d) solve problems that are quantitative in nature e) make efficient use of information resources and technology for personal and professional needs 2. **Critical Thinking** (Definition: The ability of students to analyze carefully and logically information and ideas from multiple perspectives.) Outcomes: This skill is demonstrated by the ability of students to: a) analyze complex issues and make informed decisions b) synthesize information in order to arrive at reasoned conclusions c) evaluate the logic, validity, and relevance of data d) solve challenging problems e) use knowledge and understanding to generate and explore new questions

continued on next page

Chism, N.V.N. (2007*). Peer Review of Teaching: A Sourcebook*. Bolton, MA: Anker.

Instructional Design and Development Guidelines for Teams Developing IUPUI JumpStart Courses	
The undergraduate course focuses on one or more of the following Principles of Undergraduate Learning (*cont.*):	**3. Integration and Application of Knowledge** (Definition: The ability of students to use information and concepts from studies in multiple disciplines in their intellectual, professional, and community lives.) Outcomes: This skill is demonstrated by the ability of students to apply knowledge to: a) enhance their personal lives b) meet professional standards and competencies c) further the goals of society **4. Intellectual Depth, Breadth, and Adaptiveness** (Definition: The ability of students to examine and organize disciplinary ways of knowing and to apply them to specific issues and problems.) Outcomes: a) intellectual depth describes the demonstration of substantial knowledge and understanding of at least one field of study b) intellectual breadth is demonstrated by the ability to compare and contrast approaches to knowledge in different disciplines c) adaptiveness is demonstrated by the ability to modify one's approach to an issue or problem based on the contexts and requirements of particular situations **5. Understanding Society and Culture** (Definition: The ability of students to recognize their own cultural traditions and to understand and appreciate the diversity of the human experience, both within the United States and internationally.) Outcomes: This skill is demonstrated by the ability to: a) compare and contrast the range of diversity and universality in human history, societies, and ways of life b) analyze and understand the interconnectedness of global and local concerns c) operate with civility in a complex social world **6. Values and Ethics** (Definition: The ability of students to make judgments with respect to individual conduct, citizenship, and aesthetics.) Outcomes: A sense of values and ethics is demonstrated by the ability of students to: a) make informed and principled choices regarding conflicting situations in their personal and public lives and to foresee the consequences of these choices b) recognize the importance of aesthetics in their personal lives and society

continued on next page

Chism, N.V.N. (2007). *Peer Review of Teaching: A Sourcebook.* Bolton, MA: Anker.

Some of the guidelines mentioned in the table on the previous pages have been adapted from the following sources:

Chickering, A. W., & Gamson, Z. F. (1987, June). Seven principles for good practice in undergraduate education. *AAHE Bulletin*, 39(7), 3–7.

Creighton University, School of Pharmacy. (2000). *Initial on-line course review process* (pp. 152–158). Omaha, NE: Author.

Davis, B. G. (1993). *Tools for teaching*. San Francisco, CA: Jossey-Bass.

Indiana University–Purdue University Indianapolis. (2001). *Teaching and learning: Principles of undergraduate learning*. Retrieved January 14, 2007, from the Indiana University–Purdue University Indianapolis, Portfolio web site: www.iport.iupui.edu/teach/teach_pul.htm

McGlynn, A. P. (2001). *Successful beginnings for college teaching: Engaging your students from the first day*. Madison, WI: Atwood.

Stephan, J. (2000). The syllabus and lesson plan. In D. E. Greive (Ed.), *Handbook II: Advanced teaching strategies for adjunct and part-time faculty* (pp. 55–62). Ann Arbor, MI: Part-Time Press.

University of Minnesota. (2006). *Syllabus tutorial*. Retrieved January 14, 2007, from the University of Minnesota, Center for Teaching and Learning web site: www1.umn.edu/ohr/teachlearn/tutorials/syllabus/

In addition to the references cited, staff and faculty from the IUPUI Center for Teaching and Learning, UITS Digital Media Services, the Office for Professional Development Office of Assessment, and the IUPUI Instructional Technology Roundtable all contributed to these guidelines.

Reprinted with permission.

Technical Guidelines for IUPUI JumpStart Course Development

1. **Page Construction**
   Pages have been constructed for cross-platform/multi-device functionality, content accessibility, and forward compatibility.

2. **Page Size**
   Page size is visually functional and determined by content.

3. **Color and Backgrounds**
   - Colors and backgrounds are supportive, rather than distracting.
   - The use of color is reinforced by other cues so that those using alternative browsing are not disadvantaged.

4. **Fonts**
   Chosen fonts lend themselves to on-screen readability.

5. **Links**
   - Links use an easily distinguishable color, use bolding, underlining, or both.
   - Links provide a clear rollover state, such as an underline and/or color change.
   - Links provide a visited state (usually another easily distinguishable color) to let the user know which links he or she has visited.

6. **Navigation**
   - Page numbers are provided.
   - Clear titling and numbering of units, modules, and other sections occurs.
   - Site structure is clear.
   - "Next" and "Previous" links are available.

7. **Plug-Ins, or Helper Applications**
   - Need for plug-ins is based on course requirements.
   - The most current versions of all plug-ins are used.

8. **General Accessibility Issues**
   - Alternate text contains a brief but thorough description of each image
   - Alternative, equivalent versions of multimedia resources are provided for users with disabilities (i.e., provide text transcripts of audio files).

9. **Security Issues**
   Site matches the level of security requested by the client in consultation with IT staff.

Chism, N.V.N. (2007). *Peer Review of Teaching: A Sourcebook*. Bolton, MA: Anker.

Peer Review Form for MERLOT

Peer reviews are performed by evaluation standards that divide the review into three dimensions: Quality of Content, Potential Effectiveness as a Teaching-Learning Tool, and Ease of Use. Each of these dimensions is evaluated separately. In addition to the written findings (review) by the reviewers, there is a rating for each of the three dimensions (1–5 stars, 5 being the highest). A review must average 3 stars (or textual equivalent) to be posted to the MERLOT site. For more details about the peer review process, evaluation standards, becoming a peer reviewer, or the rating system, see the MERLOT site (www.merlot.org).

Quality of Content

There are two general elements to quality of content:

1. Does the software present valid (correct) concepts, models, and skills?
2. Does the software present educationally significant concepts, models, and skills for the discipline?

To evaluate the validity of the content, the reviewers should rely on their expertise. To evaluate the educational significance of the content, reviews can use the following guidelines:

- Content is core curriculum within the discipline. Core curriculum topics are typically covered to some degree in the introductory classes within the discipline and/or "Everyone teaches it" and/or it is identified as a core area by the discipline's professional organizations
- Content is difficult to teach and learn.
- Content is a prerequisite for understanding more advanced material in the discipline

Potential Effectiveness as a Teaching-Learning Tool

Warning: This evaluation is the most difficult. Determining actual effectiveness requires actual use of the instructional software by real students and faculty. Evaluating potential effectiveness is asking you to judge, based on your expertise as a teacher, if the instructional software is likely to improve teaching and learning given the ways the faculty and students could use the tool.

Sometimes the instructional software being evaluated is taken out of context, making it difficult to evaluate. Remember that the value of "modules" is their ability to be re-purposed for use in different contexts. In evaluating the Potential Effectiveness for Teaching and Learning, it is critical to define the purpose of the learning materials. That is, you must contextualize your reviews. The MERLOT materials on Evaluation Standards and the Peer Review Reports emphasize this point. In performing a review, you can use the following three questions to help you define the pedagogical context:

1. What stage(s) in the learning process/cycle could the materials be used:
   - Explanation or description of the topic/stating the problem
   - Demonstration of the curriculum/exploration of the problem
   - Practice using the curriculum/analysis of the outcomes from solving the problem
   - Applying the curriculum to "new" problems/application of the outcomes to other problems
2. What is (are) the learning objective(s)? What should students be able to do after successfully learning with the materials?
3. What are the characteristics of the target learner(s)

An evaluation would be conditional on how the instructional software was used. For example, "If the faculty using tool X in a supervised lab with freshmen reviewed the content beforehand, and had the students do tasks A and B, then the software should enhance students' learning. The reasons are . . ." All these issues and more are also represented in the Learning Assignment screens in MERLOT.

There are other general elements to effectiveness as a teaching-learning tool that MERLOT asks reviewers to consider:

1. Does the interactive/media-rich presentation of material improve faculty and students' abilities to teach and learn the materials?
2. Can the use of the software be readily integrated into current curriculum and pedagogy within the discipline?
3. Can the software be used in a variety of ways to achieve teaching and learning goals?
4. Are the teaching-learning goals easy to identify?
5. Can good learning assignments for using the software application be written easily?

Chism, N.V.N. (2007). *Peer Review of Teaching: A Sourcebook.* Bolton, MA: Anker.

Ease of Use

The basic question underlying the ease of use standard is: How easy it is for teachers and students to use the software for the first time? Elements that effect ease of use include:

1. Are the labels, buttons, menus, text, and general layout of the computer interface consistent and visually distinct?
2. Does the user get trapped in the software?
3. Can the user get lost easily in the software?
4. Does the software provide feedback about the system status and the user's responses?
5. Does the software provide appropriate flexibility in its use?
6. Does the software require a lot of documentation, technical support, and/or instruction for most students to successfully use the software?
7. Does the software present information in ways that are familiar for students?
8. Does the software present information in ways that would be attractive to students?

Reprinted with permission.

Chism, N.V.N. (2007). *Peer Review of Teaching: A Sourcebook*. Bolton, MA: Anker.

MedEdPORTAL Digital and Educational Peer Review Form

The items listed here are taken from the complete form at www.aamc.org/meded/meded portal/web-peer-review-form.pdf. The form used a rating stem of 1–4 (no–yes), calling for a rating and providing a space for comment for each item.

Goals
- Intended target audience (e.g., students, residents) is identified.
- The author's description of this material is accurate and up-to-date.
- The author's description of the material includes clear goals or statement of purpose.

Preparation and Content Quality
- Content is accurate and up-to-date throughout the material.
- Citations, references, credits, and/or links are relevant.
- Citations, references, and credits are complete.

Methods: Effectiveness of Material
- Instructional/assessment methods are appropriate for the stated goals/objectives.
- Multimedia (e.g., videos) is used effectively.
- Learning activities are used effectively (e.g., learner control, navigation).
- Feedback is used effectively.
- Methods maintain learner dignity.
- Material is engaging.

Presentation and Ease of Use
- Material is easy to install.
- Application loads, launches, and executes smoothly (the material appears to have no bugs).
- Material is easy to use.
- Material offers effective help functions.
- Content is clear and well organized.
- Video quality is good.
- Audio quality is good.
- Image/illustration quality is good.
- The quality of the specimens is good (adequate staining, adequate specimen preparation, etc.).

Chism, N.V.N. (2007). *Peer Review of Teaching: A Sourcebook.* Bolton, MA: Anker.

Significance

- Material offers an innovative learning/teaching method.
- Evidence of product effectiveness is provided.
- Documentation describes how the material builds on prior work.
- Material contributes to the field.
- Material can be customized to fit a range of curricula/courses.

Reflective Critique

- Documentation includes lessons learned, future directions, or suggestions for adaptations or extensions.
- Documentation provides sufficient information to guide others in using the material(s).

Overall Rating

- One star: Does not meet minimal standards and does not contribute to the field. REJECT
- Two stars. Meets minimal standards and contributes to the field, but there are concerns. ACCEPT with Revisions
- Three stars. Meets quality standards and contributes to the field. ACCEPT
- Four stars. Is excellent overall and significantly contributes to the field. ACCEPT with ACCLAMATION

Strengths of the material:

Modifications required for publication:

Suggested revisions:

Reprinted with permission.

Chism, N.V.N. (2007). *Peer Review of Teaching: A Sourcebook.* Bolton, MA: Anker.

Chapter 8

Leadership for Teaching: Contributions to Scholarship of Teaching and Departmental Teaching Efforts

While the goal of much peer review is to improve and reward good classroom teaching, there is more to excellent teaching. This chapter focuses on leadership for teaching, both within the department and discipline as well as across disciplines. In particular, it looks at the scholarship of teaching and contributions to departmental teaching efforts. In a way, these activities can be considered research or service, and the extent to which this is true will depend somewhat on the institutional context and how such activities are defined. However, there is a clear sense in which these activities are organic to teaching, testifying to the depth of commitment, creativity, and student focus that teachers bring to their work.

Scholarship of Teaching

One of the four types of scholarship discussed in Ernest Boyer's *Scholarship Reconsidered* (1990) is the scholarship of teaching. By this, Boyer referred to activities through which faculty explore conceptions central to the teaching of their field, assess the effects of different teaching strategies on student learning in the discipline, and pose new directions for exploration. These activities are demonstrated in the daily work of teaching. Teachers' use of classroom assessment techniques (Angelo & Cross, 1993) helps them to explore systematically what prior knowledge and skills their students are bringing to the classroom, what they are learning, and how their students are attending to instructional interventions. Engaging in informal or formal classroom research projects is a sign that teachers take an interest in student learning and their own professional development. Peer reviewers working formatively can use the results of such inquiries to help make recommendations for teacher change and can also interpret the work as a signal of good teaching practice. Summatively, accounts of involvement in classroom assessment and research can be submitted by the teacher to the peer reviewer, whose function it is to evaluate this work in terms of what it says about the teacher in comparison with others.

Since the original articulation of the scholarship of teaching in Boyer (1990), the Carnegie Foundation for the Advancement of Teaching and the former American Association for Higher Education partnered in the Carnegie Academy for the Scholarship of Teaching and Learning, an ambitious and popular initiative that continues under the Carnegie Foundation's leadership (www.carnegiefoundation.org/CASTL/highered). Boyer's work was followed by *Scholarship Assessed* (Glassick, Huber, & Maeroff, 1997), which outlined characteristics central to the evaluation of any form of scholarship: 1) clear goals, 2) adequate preparation, 3) appropriate methods, 4) significant results, 5) effective presentation, and 6) reflective critique. These criteria can certainly be applied to the scholarship of teaching and learning.

Scholars writing about the scholarship of teaching and learning have drawn distinctions between types of scholarly activity on teaching. Several (e.g., Hutchings & Shulman, 1999; Smith, 2001) distinguish between scholarly teaching and the scholarship of teaching, indicating that public sharing and peer review are important elements of the latter. Hutchings and Shulman also point out that the scholarship of teaching and learning must be in a form that others can build on and must inquire into student learning. At many campuses, particularly those that emphasize their teaching mission or have faculty role specialization, the expectations for the scholarship of teaching and learning have escalated over the years.

Most frequently, this formal teaching scholarship results in papers, book chapters, seminars, or presentations at professional meetings. Examination of these works or descriptions of the events by the colleague provide the information needed for assessing the contribution. The questions in the resource materials section of this chapter may help in gathering data or evaluating data from papers and book chapters. For formative evaluation, feedback by the reviewer on areas in which the colleague can improve and areas in which the colleague already excels is in order. Summative feedback would result in a written overall assessment of the colleague's performance compared to others in the department or field.

Departmental Teaching Efforts

An additional important aspect of a faculty member's teaching performance is the extent to which he or she is engaged in collaborative efforts to improve teaching at the department, college, or university levels or within the professional associations of the discipline. Such activities might include chairing committees on various aspects of teaching or faculty development, serving in such departmental leadership roles as director of undergraduate or graduate studies, serving as a teaching assistant supervisor or mentor to new faculty, or organizing an institute or sessions on teaching at professional association conferences. Hoyt and Pallett (1999) enumerate several of these activities and include forms for assessing faculty performance on key dimensions of faculty contributions to the instructional program.

Information on this work is most likely found in the individual's curriculum vitae, but a short interview may help to augment understanding of the activities that have been undertaken and the impact they have had. The questions in the resource materials section of this chapter may help in gathering data or evaluating data from the curriculum vitae. As with other kinds of peer review, formative evaluation will consist of helping the colleague to improve and identify areas in which he or she already excels. Summative feedback would result in a written overall assessment of the colleague's performance compared to others in the department or field.

Teaching efforts not captured by classroom observation or review of course materials are also important to peer review. These include such activities as advising undergraduate and graduate students and serving as moderator for a student organization. Again, while these may be considered service rather than teaching, they are an essential part of teaching at almost all institutions, and as such, should be considered when discussing peer review of teaching. *Evaluating Teaching Effectiveness* by Braskamp, Brandenburg, and Ory (1984) is one of the few books that includes a form that can be used to assess such teaching. The resource materials section of this chapter contains another.

Resource Materials

Scholarship of Teaching and Leadership for Teaching

Questions for Assessing Quality of Scholarship of Teaching

Questions About Contributions to Teaching Leadership Efforts

Peer Review of Advising

Peer Review of Oversight of Student Research

Questions for Assessing Quality of Scholarship of Teaching

Extent of Scholarship
- What evidence is the colleague able to produce on scholarly efforts concerning teaching and learning?
- How does the quantity of these efforts compare with that of other colleagues?

Quality of Scholarship
- Do the papers, presentations, and the like show an examination of the assumptions in the teaching of the field?
- Are the questions or issues explored of importance to the discipline or college teaching and learning generally?
- Does the work show knowledge of previous scholarship on the topic? Does it build on this scholarship?
- Do the papers provide a framework for analysis of the issues, theoretical or otherwise?
- Are the methods used to explore the question appropriate and used according to the standards of the field?
- Have appropriate ethical measures (e.g., human subjects protection) been taken?
- Are the conclusions clear and warranted by the evidence or argument?
- Is the writing clear and style consistent?

Impact of Scholarship
- Has the work been endorsed or valued by others, as evidenced by publication in a peer reviewed journal or presentation through invited addresses?
- Has the work been disseminated to others in the department, college, university, or professional group?
- Has the work generated public discussion in the field or inspired students or colleagues to engage in scholarship on the teaching of the discipline?
- Has the work changed the teaching conceptions or practices in the field?

Chism, N.V.N. (2007). *Peer Review of Teaching: A Sourcebook*. Bolton, MA: Anker.

Questions About Contributions to Teaching Leadership Efforts

Extent of Involvement

- With what types of activities has the colleague been involved? (curriculum committee, education special interest group of the professional association, etc.)
- Has the colleague initiated these efforts personally?
- What role has the colleague taken in these activities (chairperson, resource person, etc.)?
- To what extent has the colleague served as a teaching mentor to new faculty or to graduate students in the department?
- How much time does the colleague devote to these activities compared to other colleagues?

Quality of Involvement

- According to others who have served on committees or other initiatives concerning teaching and learning with the colleague, has his or her contribution been helpful to the work of the committee?
- Is the colleague's name known at the department, university, or professional levels as one who is a leader with respect to teaching and learning?
- Is the colleague sought after for projects concerning teaching and learning or for mentoring?

Results of Efforts

- What improvements have resulted from the colleague's work at the department, college, university, or professional association?
- Have products or processes developed through the colleague's activities been disseminated?
- What feedback have others provided about the impact of this colleague's work on their teaching?
- What is the overall impact of the colleague's work in this area on teaching and learning at the department, college, university, or professional association levels?

Chism, N.V.N. (2007). *Peer Review of Teaching: A Sourcebook*. Bolton, MA: Anker.

Peer Review of Advising

Extent of Involvement

- How involved has the instructor been with respect to undergraduate or graduate student advising?
- Is there evidence that the instructor makes contact with prospective employers and other relevant parties when helpful in carrying out advising responsibilities?
- What kind of time commitment does the instructor make to undergraduate and graduate student advising, compared with other instructors in the academic unit?
- Does the instructor participate in seminars, activities, and projects involving students?
- Does the instructor help with efforts designed to attract students to the field?
- Does the instructor help with job placement, internship placement, nominations for awards, or placement in graduate/professional programs?

Quality of Involvement

- Is the instructor sought after as an advisor?
- Do students report that the instructor has been accessible and has supported their progress?
- Is the instructor knowledgeable about policies, curricula, career paths, and other topics needed in advising students?
- Does the instructor communicate enthusiasm for the field?

Results of Efforts

- Do students advised by this instructor prosper?
- Do students advised by this instructor make progress toward their degrees and obtain employment or seek further academic degrees upon graduation?
- Do students become attracted to work in the field as the result of this instructor's efforts?

Chism, N.V.N. (2007). *Peer Review of Teaching: A Sourcebook.* Bolton, MA: Anker.

Peer Review of Oversight of Student Research

Extent of Involvement
- What is the nature of the advisor's involvement with students?
- What is the frequency of interaction?
- What kind of time does the advisor invest in helping each undergraduate or graduate student advisee to conduct research?

Quality of Involvement
- Is the advisor accessible to students when they need help?
- Does the advisor take a close interest in student projects?
- Do interactions between instructor and students further students' knowledge of the field?
- Does the instructor provide prompt and constructive feedback on the progress of the project as well as on students' development of professional skills and knowledge?

Results of Efforts
- Is the thesis and dissertation work of graduate students done well?
- Do students of this instructor go on to publish and do research of high quality after they leave the program?
- Do students publish or present the results of their research in local, regional, national, or international venues?
- Do students win awards for their research?
- Do students get good placements (e.g., graduate/professional school, jobs, postdoctoral appointments) following their research experience?

Chism, N.V.N. (2007). *Peer Review of Teaching: A Sourcebook.* Bolton, MA: Anker.

Chapter 9

Teaching Portfolios

Since the 1980s, teaching portfolios (sometimes called dossiers) have been a mainstay of faculty life in Canadian universities. More recently, they have been introduced in the U.S., Australia, and many European universities as a way for faculty to document their teaching, both for improvement and personnel decision-making purposes. A portfolio consists of documents, photographs, videotapes, or other artifacts that describe the teaching of its composer. Teaching portfolios can concentrate on only one course or they may span much longer time periods and teaching situations. The main advantage of a portfolio is that it presents information holistically. A good portfolio is woven together by narrative commentary from the faculty member that describes the context for the documentation and presents reflections on the teaching itself. It presents multiple sources of evidence, chronicles the development of the instructor and the learning of the students, and projects a future vision.

Purposes of Teaching Portfolios

Teaching portfolios can be used to document teaching for several purposes. Perlman and McCann (1996) discuss the use of a teaching portfolio in the special case of peer review that is called into play during a faculty search. They recommend the portfolio format as a way to gather information about the teaching of candidates. The rating form that they suggest for use in peer review of candidate portfolios is reprinted in the resource materials section of this chapter.

Teaching portfolios are sometimes prepared for the purpose of teaching awards. In one study, Chism (2006) found that 14% of the teaching awards programs she explored required that the candidate submit a portfolio. About one-fifth of these programs specified the contents of the portfolio while the rest left this decision to the discretion of the candidate. Very little information was available on the process that peers used to review these portfolios; however, the portfolio can be an excellent vehicle for documenting teaching excellence when coupled with a systematic process for reviewing it. One example of a system that requires a portfolio is the Indiana University Faculty Colloquium on Excellence in Teaching (www.facet.iupui.edu/nominations/guidelines.html).

Portfolios are used more routinely in ongoing summative and formative evaluation of teaching. The most well-known summative format is the promotion and tenure dossier, prepared according to the specifications of the candidate's institution. Depending on the context, such portfolios are usually a cumulative record of the faculty member's work in rank. The teaching section generally contains a candidate statement, information on teaching and advising loads, teaching evaluations (often from self, students, and peers), available evidence on teaching impact, and documentation of awards, service, and scholarship regarding teaching and learning. Peers often have guidelines for review, but these vary in their specificity. In some cases, the guidelines contain clear standards and in others, the basis for judgment is not stipulated. Research on portfolio judgments (Centra, 2000; Root, 1987) indicates that consensus among reviewers about the standards and methods of review of such dossiers increases the reliability greatly. The forms for summative portfolios in the resource materials section of this chapter can be adapted for such purposes.

Portfolios are also used for formative evaluation of teaching. Recently, special attention has been placed on the course portfolio. Even though this format concentrates on a single course, it allows the author to present an in-depth look at that course, revealing much about the teaching philosophy, creativity, and impact of the faculty member. The former American Association for Higher Education project on peer review of teaching (Hutchings, 1998) issued a helpful manual for the construction of course portfolios. Bernstein (2002) led a national project on course portfolios, involving peer review of these portfolios across five institutions. In both projects, the emphasis was on student learning and the teacher as inquirer into the facilitation of learning.

In a recent work, Bernstein, Burnett, Goodburn, and Savory (2006) frame their treatment of peer review of teaching around the course portfolio. They distinguish between the benchmark portfolio and the inquiry portfolio. The *benchmark portfolio* focuses on the current state of student learning in a course and documents teaching practices for further investigation. An *inquiry portfolio* looks at a course over time to assess the impact of teaching practices and changes in student learning. Both are intended mainly for formative purposes, but can be used summatively, and the role of peer review is quite important in either case. Guidelines for course portfolio review from Bernstein et al. follow the recommended structure of the course portfolio and are reprinted in the resource materials section of this chapter.

A new development made possible by technology is the electronic faculty portfolio, available through commercial or institutional products (see, for example, Woodroof & Searcy, 2004, or selected chapters in Jafari & Kaufman, 2006). These systems consist of repositories with a user interface that allows faculty members to store and retrieve documents and artifacts about their work in much the same way as a print portfolio does, with several added advantages. The advantages of these systems include the convenience to the faculty member and access for the peer reviewer. Institutional data on course offerings taught by a given instructor, course evaluation results, or a variety of other data can be imported into the portfolio, saving the faculty member from compiling this information. The faculty member can also attach files in any format, such as video or audio, and can provide links to additional information, such as to student projects or course materials. Once entered, these forms of documentation can be retrieved in a variety of formats, saving the faculty member from reformatting or repeatedly entering the same data for different purposes. Peer reviewers, when given access to all or a specified part of the portfolio, can explore among the layers of evidence from their own desktop, whether they are on the same campus or not, without the exchange of stacks of paper. Reviewers can easily find the information that best answers their questions about the teaching performance, and depending on the system in use, may also enter their review as part of the record. Electronic portfolios can be used for many purposes, from career development planning to reflective journaling and the more common uses of documenting performance for annual review or promotion and tenure decisions.

Contents of Teaching Portfolios

Several books describe the items that can be included a teaching portfolio. Lists can be found in Centra (2000), Knapper and Wright (2001), Murray (1995), O'Neil and Wright (1995), Seldin (2004), and Shore et al. (1986). The following list contains items that are usually mentioned:

- Description of teaching responsibilities (including advising and other work)
- Statement of teaching philosophy and goals

- Representative course syllabi
- Samples of course handouts and tests
- Self-evaluation statement
- Description of course development or teaching improvement efforts
- Copies of papers or presentations on teaching topics
- Videotape of classroom teaching
- Records of teaching awards and honors
- Summaries of student evaluations of teaching
- Reports of peers who have observed class
- Comments of others who have reviewed course materials
- Comments of those who know about the instructor's teaching contributions to the department or field
- Samples of student work (preferably graded)

Bass (2000) recounts his compilation of a hypertext course portfolio, arguing that within an electronic environment faculty can use such innovative approaches to representing teaching as "multimedia case study analyses, teacher-scholar webs that link faculty teaching work over time, collective digital archives of teaching materials, and reflections where faculty connect their work in courses to other cohort courses in local, disciplinary, and national contexts" (p. 45).

Bernstein's (2002, pp. 218–219) description of the contents of a course portfolio focuses on faculty reflection on the documentation. For example, as faculty comment on the course syllabus, they are to address the following questions:

Course Goals and Rationale
- What do you want students to learn from your course?
  — What do you want them to know? What do you want them to be able to do? What do you want them to understand? What perspectives or attitudes do you want them to have?
  — What is important for them to learn about your field? What should they learn about themselves as students or contributors to our society?
- Why did you choose the goals you did?
  — Why is it necessary for your students to achieve these goals? What do you know about your students that makes these goals appropriate for their education?
  — What perspectives of your discipline or field shaped your goals for the course? How did you decide between the breadth and depth of content? How is the depth of understanding reflected in your course goals?

- Where are these goals found in the syllabus for your course?
    — What readings or other sources of material are connected with the particular goals of the course? How did your vision of the course influence your selection of topics and resources?
    — Are there any activities for students in the syllabus that are particularly crafted to achieve individual goals of the course?

Sets of questions prompt the faculty member to reflect on teaching methods, course materials, course activities, and the nature of student understanding. In the case of the course portfolio, then, the documentation may include many of the standard items in a teaching portfolio, but they pertain to only one course, and the reflection is much more extensive than in the usual teaching portfolio.

Those who write about teaching portfolios emphasize that they should not contain raw data, should use a variety of kinds of evidence and existing assessment data when possible, and that the faculty member should be purposeful about selecting evidence about student learning (Bernstein, 1998, 2002; Bernstein et al., 2006; Centra, 2000; Knapper & Wright, 2001; Seldin, 1994).

Reviewing Teaching Portfolios

Peer review of teaching portfolios corresponds to the purpose of the portfolio. When a portfolio is being assembled for formative purposes, the peer reviewer's role is to give advice, not only on teaching development, but on the construction of the portfolio itself. The reviewer can appraise the portfolio through the eyes of others who will ultimately review it for decision-making. The peer is acting in a mentor role in this function, helping the instructor to select those documents that are most descriptive of the teaching as well as reading and providing suggestions on the narrative that the instructor uses to situate the course syllabus, handout samples, summaries of student evaluations, or other items in the portfolio. The focus advised by many writers is on student learning first, and second, in an integral way, on the facilitation of that learning. The conversation is a collegial exchange about the end goals of the teaching and to what extent they were achieved as evidenced by student learning. The puzzles, successes, and disappointments of the learning results are the gist of the conversation, leading to ideas for future modes of facilitating learning. These conversations are powerful forms of assistance to the faculty member using the portfolio for improvement purposes. Several institutions use the construction of a portfolio as the occasion for collaborative faculty development. Teachers come together to discuss a given portfolio component, such as syllabi or summaries of student ratings or teaching philosophy statements, for the purpose of common reflections and exploration of assumptions.

When a portfolio is used summatively, the peer reviewer is in the position of making a judgment on the overall quality of the teaching as evidenced by the portfolio. As indicated above, reviews of teaching portfolios for summative purposes have not been without problems. Several studies point out problems with reliability of ratings. Centra (1975), who did one of the primary studies, concludes that it is important to consider carefully how reviewers are selected, that the portfolio should include actual work samples rather than only reflective statements or summaries of judgments of others, and that reviewers should receive training in evaluating portfolios according to agreed-upon criteria. In a later work, Centra (2000) cites a study by Root (1987) that found high reliability of peer review of a teaching portfolio when the reviewing panel consisted of at least members who had discussed standards and criteria prior to their review. Braskamp and Ory (1994) recommend that several colleagues, each using a list of specific criteria, review the portfolio independent of each other. They further make the following recommendations (p. 236):

- Institutional records that are collected periodically and systematically will provide the most comprehensive profiles of performance over the career of a faculty member.
- Actual work samples enhance the authenticity of portfolios.
- Faculty need freedom to organize their records and evidence to reflect their unique contributions. A balance between individuality and campus standardization is necessary.
- Faculty should be given an opportunity to view the results of the document to correct any factual errors.
- Faculty can be given examples of portfolios to help them prepare their own.
- Consultants, especially faculty experienced with portfolios, can help faculty prepare and review their portfolios.
- Guidelines should be provided to course material reviewers to increase interrater reliability.

Although it is important that the academic unit reach agreement on a set of criteria to use in reviewing portfolios, some general criteria are listed next for consideration.

COMPLETENESS

Is the portfolio thorough? Does it contain enough evidence to judge the quality of the teaching?

Consistency

Do the materials submitted show that there is a match between what the instructor says are goals and the actions taken in teaching? For example, do the statements in the philosophy of teaching correspond with the implicit philosophy in the syllabus, tests, and handouts or in the classroom teaching described on the peer observation record?

Reflection

Does the instructor show a thoughtfulness about teaching through the inclusion of self-evaluation materials, philosophy of teaching statements, goal statements, and commentary on the portfolio documents? Does this reflection offer insights into the context of the documents in the portfolio, the instructor's efforts to improve, the vision for the future?

Quality

Does the portfolio show improvement in teaching and learning over time? Do the documents and other products portray a teacher whose work is exemplary in the field? Compared to other portfolios, does this portfolio show that students and peers rate the teaching highly? Does the overall portfolio show innovation, experimentation, accuracy of content, and other desirable characteristics?

Credibility and Reliability

Is the assembled evidence well rounded and detailed, rather than one-sided? Are the judgments of peers, students, and others included in the portfolio documentation in agreement? Is there a balance among the sources of evidence that includes the self, students, and peers?

Examples of systems for evaluating teaching portfolios are in Seldin (1993b) and in the resource materials section of this chapter.

Resource Materials
Teaching Portfolios

Review of Portfolios Intended for Improvement Purposes

Review of Course Portfolios

Review of Portfolios Intended for Hiring Decisions

Review of Portfolios Intended for Ongoing Summative Purposes
(Narrative Version)

Review of Portfolios Intended for Ongoing Summative Purposes
(Rating Form Version)

Review of Portfolios Intended for Improvement Purposes

Ideally, feedback on a portfolio that is compiled for purposes of improvement is exchanged during personal conversations. However, when the reviewer is at a distance, or in-person meetings or phone calls are not feasible, written feedback may be the only practical way to respond. The items below are based on the criteria presented earlier (completeness, consistency, reflection, quality, credibility, and reliability) and can be used to prepare oral feedback as well as to provide a written response. These items look at the overall portfolio, assuming that the feedback forms presented in earlier chapters or those in Richlin (2006) might be used to assess different components of the portfolio, such as the syllabus and course materials.

1. Does the portfolio contain the type and amount   Yes   No
    of information needed to address the instructor's
    concerns about his or her teaching?

    If so, what do the materials tell you about these concerns?

    If not, what other materials would be helpful?

2. Looking over the materials that are assembled, are there   Yes   No
    clear connections between espoused intentions (course
    goal statements, philosophy statements) and actual practices
    (assessment measures, syllabus format)?

    If so, what good connections are in evidence?

    If not, what things need to be aligned?

3. Does the portfolio contain reflective statements by the   Yes   No
    instructor that show engagement with the central teaching
    issues? Is there enough context provided so that the reviewer
    knows how to evaluate the information?

    If so, what are your responses to these reflections?

    If not, what questions might the instructor think and write about?

    What might help the instructor to be reflective?

Chism, N.V.N. (2007). *Peer Review of Teaching: A Sourcebook*. Bolton, MA: Anker.

4. Is the portfolio organized in such a way as to show   Yes   No
    improvement?

    If so, what changes do you note?

    If not, how can the instructor best improve the organization
    of the portfolio to be able to see patterns over time?

5. Has the instructor drawn on other sources of opinion   Yes   No
    and evidence in compiling the portfolio?

    If so, what patterns do you note across the assembled evidence?

    If not, how can the instructor collect multiple kinds of data?

6. Overall, are there other ways in which the instructor should   Yes   No
    work with the portfolio concept for the improvement of
    teaching, such as compiling a course portfolio, reviewing
    and revising regularly, or the like?

    If so, what recommendations would you make?

7. Are certain items in this portfolio suitable for use in   Yes   No
    a summative portfolio?

    If so, which ones?

    If not, what items would better demonstrate teaching
    effectiveness when decision-making is the purpose?

Chism, N.V.N. (2007). *Peer Review of Teaching: A Sourcebook.* Bolton, MA: Anker.

Review of Course Portfolios

When considering a course portfolio, peer reviewers are engaging in dialogue about a particular context of teaching and learning. Since depth of understanding is sought, it is often best for the reviewer to be a person who has taught or is teaching a similar course. Often, these reviews are done over distance (since a match with the special course area is sought) and often for formative purposes and advancement of the scholarship of teaching. Bernstein, Burnett, Goodburn, and Savory's (2006, pp. 130–131) guidelines for reviewers parallel the structure of the guidelines for course portfolio authors and are reprinted below.

Intellectual content of the course

Please evaluate the quality of the *course's intellectual content*. This may include but is not limited to:

- Appropriateness of course material both for the curriculum and the institution
- Intellectual coherence of course content
- Articulation of intellectual goals for learners and congruence of those goals with course content and mission
- Value or relevance of ideas, knowledge, and skills covered by the course

Quality of teaching practices

Please evaluate the *quality of the teaching practices* used in the course. This may include but is not limited to:

- Organization and planning of contact time; congruence between planned and actual use of contact time
- Opportunities to actively engage students in the material
- Opportunities (in or out of class) for students to practice the skills embedded in the course goals
- Particularly creative or effective uses of contact time that seem likely to improve student understanding
- Activities scheduled outside of contact time that contribute to student achievement (this may include extracurricular activities, group projects, electronic discussions, or any other planned course-related assignments or activities)
- Course structures or procedures that contribute especially to the likely achievement of understanding by learners

Chism, N.V.N. (2007). *Peer Review of Teaching: A Sourcebook*. Bolton, MA: Anker.

Quality of student understanding

Please evaluate the *quality of student understanding*. This may include but is not limited to:

- Appropriateness of student performance, in light of course goals, course level, and institution
- Performance levels that reflect challenging levels of conceptual understanding and critical evaluation of the material appropriate to the level of the course and of the students
- Appropriateness of forms of evaluation and assessment, given the stated goals of the course
- Creativity in providing students with ways to demonstrate their understanding of and ability to use the ideas and content of the course
- Alignment between the weighting of course assignments in grade calculation with the relative importance of the course goals
- Demonstration by an appropriate percentage of students that they are achieving competence in the stated course goals, or identification of reasons why they might not be reaching these levels of competence
- Revisions or modifications to the course that could improve performance

Evidence of reflection and development

Please evaluate the *evidence of reflection and development*. This may include but is not limited to:

- Substantive reflection by the faculty member on the achievement of the goals for the course
- Identification of any meaningful relations between teaching practice and student performance
- Evidence of changed teaching practice over successive course offerings in reaction to prior student understanding
- Evidence of insightful analysis of teaching practice that resulted from consideration of student performance

Reprinted with permission.

Chism, N.V.N. (2007). *Peer Review of Teaching: A Sourcebook*. Bolton, MA: Anker.

Review of Portfolios Intended for Hiring Decisions

Perlman and McCann (1996, p. 81) provide an example of a portfolio rating form intended for use in evaluating the teaching of a candidate for a faculty position.

Candidate Name _____

Complete Portfolio   Yes   No

	Poor	Fair	Good	Very Good	Excellent
Core Areas					
Candidate Teaching Statement	1	2	3	4	5
Depth and Expertise	1	2	3	4	5
Breadth	1	2	3	4	5
Teacher Preparation and Experience	1	2	3	4	5
Instructional Materials and Feedback	1	2	3	4	5
Development as a Teacher	1	2	3	4	5
Other Important Criteria					
Instructional Activity Outside the Classroom	1	2	3	4	5
Overall Ratings					
Fit for Position	1	2	3	4	5
Teaching Abilities and Potential	1	2	3	4	5

Remarks—Other Information Needed

Reprinted with permission.

Chism, N.V.N. (2007). *Peer Review of Teaching: A Sourcebook.* Bolton, MA: Anker.

Review of Portfolios Intended for Ongoing Summative Purposes (Narrative Version)

In reviewing a portfolio for summative purposes, the focus is not on the process dimensions of assembling a portfolio, but rather on what the evidence says about the effectiveness of the portfolio author's teaching and how this compares with the teaching of others. Thus, the review of each of the portfolio components (syllabus, course materials, and the like) should be done individually, using the kinds of instruments in the previous resource sections or alternative systematic procedures that are in place for these reviews. These evaluations of the individual components form the basis for an overall evaluation.

Prior to the time of a summative portfolio review, instructors should receive clear directions about what the portfolio should contain and how it will be judged. At the time of the review, peers should have standard and systematic procedures for undertaking the review. Traditionally, the review process has consisted of a group conversation, followed by a letter summarizing that conversation. While such narrative feedback may be the option of choice in a given situation, it should be based on articulated criteria and standards. A set of open-ended questions that will guide the reviewer's narrative will help to provide better reliability than this approach has had to date. The questions might include:

- Does this instructor possess a broad, deep, and current knowledge of the content, as demonstrated by the course syllabi, bibliographies, assignments, handouts, and tests in the portfolio? Is there previous peer testimony about this knowledge through reports of classroom visits, review of materials, or the like?
- Does the instructor use good design principles to facilitate learning in the courses taught, as demonstrated by the teaching philosophy statement and course materials?
- Does the instructor deliver effective instruction, as indicated by summaries of previous student evaluations of instruction, reports by peers, and review of the products of student learning, such as tests, papers, and project reports?
- Has the instructor shown effectiveness in non-classroom teaching roles, such as student advising and supervision of student research, as demonstrated by student testimony, student progress, and the products of student learning?
- Does the instructor invest in teaching development and engage in the scholarship of teaching, as demonstrated by the teaching philosophy statement; the record of teaching leadership efforts inside the department and externally; and the record of publication, presentation, and conference participation in the teaching of the discipline?

Chism, N.V.N. (2007). *Peer Review of Teaching: A Sourcebook*. Bolton, MA: Anker.

- Has the instructor contributed extensively to the teaching mission of the department, as indicated by the record of teaching responsibilities, both through formal courses, non-classroom teaching, and course development?
- Overall, what is the quality of teaching documented in this portfolio and what recommendation do we make on this personnel decision?

Chism, N.V.N. (2007). *Peer Review of Teaching: A Sourcebook*. Bolton, MA: Anker.

Review of Portfolios Intended for Ongoing Summative Purposes (Rating Form Version)

Instead of a narrative report, reviewers can use a summative rating form that illustrates the judgment process more specifically. The form should originate in discussions within the academic unit about its priorities and standards. To put together such an overall evaluation form, raters must first determine the following:

- The areas in which the instructor will be assessed
- The evidence that will be used to decide each area
- The relative weight of each of the areas
- The criteria for excellence
- The rating scale

Areas of Teaching and Evidence

The areas should be broad, since an overall assessment is being sought. Portfolio evidence suitable to each area should be listed. Possibilities include:

Evidence of content expertise. To what extent do these materials show that the instructor has a broad, deep, and current knowledge of the content he or she is teaching?
- Course syllabi
- Course reading list/bibliography
- Course assignments
- Course handouts and visuals
- Tests
- Reports of classroom visits by peers

Evidence of instructional design expertise. To what extent does the portfolio show that the instructor uses good design principles to facilitate learning in the courses taught?
- Philosophy of teaching statement
- Course syllabi
- Course assignments
- Course handouts
- Tests

Expertise in instructional delivery. To what extent does the instructor deliver effective instruction, both in the classroom and outside?
- Evidence
- Reports of student ratings of instruction
- Reports of classroom visits by peers

Chism, N.V.N. (2007). *Peer Review of Teaching: A Sourcebook.* Bolton, MA: Anker.

- Review of products of student learning (papers, tests, project reports)
- Reports of advisee opinion and progress

Expertise in teaching development and scholarship. To what extent does the portfolio demonstrate that the instructor invests in teaching improvement activities and participates in the scholarship of teaching in his or her field?
- Philosophy of teaching statement
- Report of teaching leadership efforts within the department, institution, professional association, nation, or world
- Record of publication, presentation, and conference participation in the area of teaching within the discipline or generally

Evidence of involvement in teaching. How extensive is the instructor's record?
- Record of teaching responsibilities, including course development
- Record of advising and other non-classroom teaching responsibilities

Relative Weight of Each Area

A conversation about the value placed on each area identified relative to the whole should result in some consensus about these values. Arreola (2007) provides extensive advice for developing weighting schemes. For the above categories, for example, the scheme might look like this:

Content expertise	30%
Instructional design expertise	20%
Expertise in instructional delivery	30%
Teaching development and scholarship	10%
Involvement in teaching	10%

Criteria for Excellence and Rating Scale

Within each category, peers should come to some agreement about what criteria will be used to determine excellence and how these will be reflected in a rating scheme. For the above categories, for example, the following criteria might be used to assess content expertise.

Content expertise

Factual accuracy:	Extremely accurate 3	Some errors noted 2	Inaccurate 1
Breadth of knowledge:	Extremely broad 3	Somewhat broad 2	Very narrow 1
Depth of knowledge:	Extremely deep 3	Somewhat deep 2	Very superficial 1
Currency:	Cutting edge 3	Somewhat current 2	Outdated 1

Chism, N.V.N. (2007). *Peer Review of Teaching: A Sourcebook*. Bolton, MA: Anker.

Explanatory comments:

Putting It All Together

When the above criteria have been determined, the final form can contain a tabulation section that lists the areas, the instructor's score for each area, the weight for each area, and the instructor's total score. The scores for a given instructor can then be compared with those of other instructors in making personnel decisions. Context must be considered in making these comparisons. A place for decision rendered is often added. Summary written comments are optional, but desirable. A total section might look like this:

Total

	Instructor's Rating	×	Weight	=	Score
Content expertise	_____	×	.30		_____
Instructional design expertise	_____	×	.20		_____
Expertise in instructional delivery	_____	×	.30		_____
Teaching development and scholarship	_____	×	.10		_____
Involvement in teaching	_____	×	.10		_____

Total score out of a possible _____ points:

Comparison to norm/previous scores:

Considerably higher	Slightly higher	Average	Slightly lower	Considerably lower

Recommendation: (Promote, salary increase, etc.)

Summary statement:

Chism, N.V.N. (2007). *Peer Review of Teaching: A Sourcebook*. Bolton, MA: Anker.

Chapter 10

Summary

Although this volume has focused in some detail on the development of systematic processes for peer review of teaching, a primary consideration to the effectiveness of any peer review process is more overarching and less practical—an attitude of professionalism that respects both the individual colleague and the profession of college teaching itself. When peer review is undertaken as an activity that is critical to the well-being of one's profession and one's institution and regarded as an opportunity to provide a colleague with developmental direction, it requires certain "habits of the heart":

- *Peer review of teaching must be perceived as a valuable activity, even though it is not directed to one's own specific interests and purposes.* It requires an appreciation for a larger mission than one's own in order to devote time to the development of another person and to the quality of one's profession. It also requires the type of vision that enables one to see why this investment is ultimately very beneficial.
- *Peer review of teaching must be seen as both compassionate and principled.* Accomplishing the work of college teaching is not easy; there are rigorous standards of performance that must be upheld. On the other hand, helping others appreciate the complexity of teaching and rise to the challenge of teaching well requires patience and understanding.
- *Peer review of teaching requires generosity of spirit.* It calls on the reviewer to put aside rivalries, bad memories, self-interest, and petty likes and dislikes in order to be fair

to another. Reviewers also need to be open-minded regarding different approaches; they may need to overlook habits that they find annoying or turf issues that are present as they conduct reviews.

- *Peer review of teaching requires patience and attention to detail.* The work of examining graded papers, observing classes, and reading philosophies of teaching might not be highly compelling tasks to most academics, yet in order for peer review to yield good results, these tasks must be done carefully and thoughtfully.

- *Peer review of teaching requires an attitude of intellectual and professional curiosity.* This work raises issues that are troublesome for the reviewer, issues such as: What do grades mean? What are the central structures of this discipline? What do students need to know? It is important that a reviewer be able to embrace and struggle with these issues in order to approach the work with the depth it demands as well as to enable growth through the process.

- *Peer review of teaching requires creativity.* Especially when used formatively, peer review can be embedded in various situations designed to make it most effective. Asking faculty to identify their most and least favorite kind of student opens up windows for exploration; generating new ways of analyzing and presenting data can help colleagues see interesting parallels and contradictions in students' and faculty members' comments about their teaching behaviors.

- *Peer review requires courage.* It is not easy to be honest with our peers, and it is often uncomfortable to stand in judgment. In the case of summative peer review, consequences of the peer reviewer's decisions can be dramatic. In formative peer review, conversations can touch on issues very sensitive to the colleague and will require honesty and commitment to complete.

- *Peer review requires that reviewers be willing to grow themselves.* Evaluating others' work means being open-minded to possibilities and practices that are different from one's own. It necessitates much reflection about criteria and often will call for testing taken-for-granted assumptions and routines in light of differences.

Developing a Set of Principles

Just as it is important to develop peer review practices that set out criteria, activities, and timelines, it is advantageous to think more philosophically about the process as a whole. The "habits of the heart" just listed might serve as a springboard for a given academic unit to discuss its hopes and commitments toward peer review. Although it might be a good exercise to develop this vision at the beginning of peer review activity, lessons learned during the first phases of implementation can add to or inspire such a document and enhance its authenticity.

One sample of a statement comes from the developers of a project on peer review training and education in the College of Letters and Science at the University of Wisconsin–Oshkosh. Professors Baron Perlman and Lee McCann enumerated the following guiding principles for their project on the peer review of teaching.

GUIDING PRINCIPLES FOR QUALITY PEER REVIEW OF TEACHING

Whether a peer review of teaching includes classroom visits, a teaching portfolio, or a more limited submission of teaching materials (e.g., syllabi), there are certain general principles to be aware of.

1. Knowing and understanding a subject does not mean you can teach it. Good teachers are made, not born.
2. Considerable thought and effort is needed for good peer review. The unit needs to give thought to its criteria and process: The reviewers and those being reviewed will contribute significant time and effort. A review involves gathering data, insight by both reviewer and teacher, and helpful feedback.
3. The notion of "to sit beside" is critical. As described by Braskamp and Ory (1994):

> "To sit beside" brings to mind such verbs as to engage, to involve, to interact, to share, to trust. It conjures up team learning, working together, discussing, reflecting, helping, building, collaboration. It makes one think of cooperative learning, community, communication, coaching, caring, and consultation. When two people "sit beside" each other, engaged in assessing, one may very well be judging and providing feedback about the other's performance, but the style and context of the exchange is critical. "Sitting beside" implies dialogue and discourse, with one person trying to understand the other's perspective before giving value judgments. Describing and understanding precede judging, but consensus is not the goal. (p. 13)

Peer review does not involve a non-expert consulting with or being acted upon by an expert. The most successful peer review processes of teaching are collaborative. Such peer review involves:

- Helping and building, not judging
- Two professionals working with each other on teaching
- Engagement, collaboration, and reflection

- Dialogue and discourse
- Describing and understanding—the ultimate goal is better teaching

4. Peer review focuses on the thinking behind the work—faculty members' reasons for teaching the way they do, as well as the actual work itself. Teachers being reviewed need to give thought to their approaches to teaching.

5. Good peer review involves being tough on the issues but tender on the person.

6. Unit guidelines and processes must allow for presentation and review of more than classroom teaching: i.e., the advising, supervising, guiding, and mentoring of students; developing learning activities, such as designing or redesigning courses and unit curricula; and development as a teacher.

7. Discourse is to be based on reasoned options, not personal biases or judgments. A good peer review requires reflection by the reviewee on their teaching and course materials, and by the reviewers on what they have read, discussed, and experienced.

8. Reviewers also benefit from peer review.

9. There should be no surprises. Faculty must know how a peer review will be used. Everyone in a unit must know the process and criteria as clearly set forth. The reviewer and teacher must agree on the process of peer review. Confidentiality in a formative review must be maintained. For example, the literature supports visiting a class by invitation only. Yes, you may get the teacher's best effort, but since there should be multiple sources of assessment of teaching (e.g., student evaluations, portfolio, materials), the unit will learn if this best effort (assuming it is passable) is representative.

10. Peer review focuses on specific teaching behaviors (e.g., syllabi, handouts, organization of lecture, eliciting questions from students, level of content).

11. Build on strengths. It is easy to pick out what needs work. First identify what went well and only then offer feedback about what might be worked on so the faculty member's teaching improves.

12. Feedback must be provided in a timely and thoughtful manner. The reviewer should meet with the faculty member being reviewed to provide this feedback (even when college-wide peer review is ongoing). This conversation should be followed by written feedback when summative review is taking place. Remain available for assistance in the future. Your feedback may be needed again at a later date.

13. Do no harm. Peer review can be anxiety producing and difficult for both reviewer and reviewee. Reviewers may worry that their findings may cause someone to be denied tenure, or be made public and cause dissension and disagreement, and

that they were not sensitive enough to the self-esteem and feelings of the faculty member who is being reviewed. The person being reviewed, whether for summative or formative purposes, may be concerned about being found inadequate or less than excellent, or of being treated unfairly or harshly. Trust and collaboration minimize the potential for harm and maximize positive outcomes such as better teaching.

14. Be patient. Changing unit or institutional culture and climate toward a systematic peer review process can be slow and difficult. Those being reviewed need time to adjust to the idea and the process. Those doing the reviewing need time to improve their skills and learn how to work with colleagues on teaching-related issues.

15. Peer review takes time. The process is often more time-consuming than other approaches that many faculty are currently using. Yet the sense of contributing to teaching development and working with colleagues usually makes the additional responsibility and time commitment worthwhile. There are no easy responses to comments about the time peer review demands.

Review

The following steps toward the development of a peer review system have been enumerated in this volume:

1. Obtaining commitment
2. Assigning leadership responsibility
3. Developing a statement that specifies:
   - Who will be included
   - What purposes peer review will serve
   - What areas of teaching will be reviewed
   - What criteria will be specified
   - What standards will be used
   - How the evidence will be collected
   - What process will be used for assessing the evidence
   - How feedback will be provided/judgments documented
4. Developing guiding principles
5. Assigning oversight responsibility
6. Allocating resources
7. Communicating the plan
8. Implementing the system
9. Periodically assessing and revising the system

Peer review provides an opportunity for dialogue and reflection on teaching that not many other activities afford. While it doubtless adds to the time commitments of an already overcommitted faculty, it is too valuable and important to neglect. As an essential activity directed toward the development of college teachers and the effectiveness of the teaching profession in higher education, peer review must be the cornerstone of future faculty evaluation methods.

Useful Sources

Arreola, R. A. (2007). *Developing a comprehensive faculty evaluation system: A guide to designing, building, and operating large-scale faculty evaluation systems* (3rd ed.). Bolton, MA: Anker.

Bernstein, D., Burnett, A. N., Goodburn, A., & Savory, P. (2006). *Making teaching and learning visible: Course portfolios and the peer review of teaching.* Bolton, MA: Anker.

Bernstein, D., & Quinlan, K. M. (Eds.). (1996, Spring). The peer review of teaching [Special issue]. *Innovative Higher Education, 20*(4).

Braskamp, L. A., & Ory, J. C. (1994). *Assessing faculty work: Enhancing individual and institutional performance.* San Francisco, CA: Jossey-Bass.

Centra, J. A. (1993). *Reflective faculty evaluation: Enhancing teaching and determining faculty effectiveness.* San Francisco, CA: Jossey-Bass.

French-Lazovik, G. (1981). Peer review: Documentary evidence in the evaluation of teaching. In J. Millman (Ed.), *Handbook of teacher evaluation* (pp. 73–89). Thousand Oaks, CA: Sage.

Hutchings, P. (Ed.). (1995). *From idea to prototype: The peer review of teaching: A project workbook.* Sterling, VA: Stylus.

Hutchings, P. (1996). *Making teaching community property: A menu for peer collaboration and peer review.* Sterling, VA: Stylus.

Keig, L., & Waggoner, M. D. (1994). *Collaborative peer review: The role of faculty in improving college teaching* (ASHE-ERIC Higher Education Report No. 2). Washington, DC: The George Washington University, Graduate School of Education and Human Development.

Leaming, D. R. (2007). *Academic leadership: A practical guide to chairing the department* (2nd ed.). Bolton, MA: Anker.

Murray, J. P. (1995). *Successful faculty development and evaluation: The complete teaching portfolio* (ASHE-ERIC Higher Education Report No. 8). Washington, DC: The George Washington University, Graduate School of Education and Human Development.

Pritchard, R. D., Watson, M. D., Kelly, K., & Paquin, A. R. (1998). *Helping teachers teach well: A new system for measuring and improving teaching effectiveness in higher education*. Lanham, MD: Lexington Books.

Richlin, L., & Cox, M. (Eds.). (1995). Special focus: Evaluation of teaching [Special issue]. *Journal on Excellence in College Teaching, 6*(3).

Ryan, K. E. (Ed.). (2000). *New directions for teaching and learning: No. 83. Evaluating teaching in higher education: A vision for the future*. San Francisco, CA: Jossey-Bass.

Seldin, P., & Associates. (1995). *Improving college teaching*. Bolton, MA: Anker.

Seldin, P., & Associates. (2006). *Evaluating faculty performance: A practical guide to assessing teaching, research, and service*. Bolton, MA: Anker.

Weimer, M. (1990). *Improving college teaching: Strategies for developing instructional effectiveness*. San Francisco, CA: Jossey-Bass.

Wright, W. A., & Associates. (1995). *Teaching improvement practices: Successful strategies for higher education*. Bolton, MA: Anker.

References

Angelo, T. A. (1996). Relating exemplary teaching to student learning. In M. D. Svinicki & R. J. Menges (Eds.), *New directions for teaching and learning, No. 65. Honoring exemplary teaching* (pp. 57–64). San Francisco, CA: Jossey-Bass.

Angelo, T. A., & Cross, K. P. (1993). *Classroom assessment techniques: A handbook for college teachers* (2nd ed.). San Francisco, CA: Jossey-Bass.

Arreola, R. A. (2007). *Developing a comprehensive faculty evaluation system: A guide to designing, building, and operating large-scale faculty evaluation systems* (3rd ed.). Bolton, MA: Anker.

Barrett, H. D. (2001). Electronic portfolio = multimedia development + portfolio development: Electronic portfolio development process. In B. L. Cambridge (Ed.), *Electronic portfolios: Emerging practices in student, faculty, and institutional learning* (pp. 110–116). Sterling, VA: Stylus.

Bass, R. (2000). Technology, evaluation, and the visibility of teaching and learning. In K. E. Ryan (Ed.), *New directions for teaching and learning: No. 83. Evaluating teaching in higher education: A vision for the future* (pp. 35–50). San Francisco, CA: Jossey-Bass.

Batista, E. (1976, September). The place of colleague evaluation in the appraisal of college teaching: A review of the literature. *Research in Higher Education, 4*(3), 257–271.

Beckman, T. J. (2004, April). Lessons learned from a peer review of bedside teaching. *Academic Medicine, 79*(4), 343–346.

Beckman, T. J., Ghosh, A. K., Cook, D. A., Erwin, P. J., & Mandrekar, J. N. (2004, September). How reliable are assessments of clinical teaching? A review of the published instruments. *Journal of General Internal Medicine, 19*(9), 971–977.

Beckman, T. J., Lee, M. C., Rohren, C. H., & Pankratz, V. S. (2003, March). Evaluating an instrument for the peer review of inpatient teaching. *Medical Teacher, 25*(2), 131–135.

Bellman, L. (2004, June). A qualitative evaluation of senior house officers' teaching and learning: Towards sharing good practice. *Medical Teacher, 26*(4), 313–320.

Bergquist, W., & Phillips, S. (1995). *Developing human and organizational resources: A comprehensive manual.* Point Arena, CA: Peter Magnusson Press.

Bernstein, D. (1996, June). A departmental system for balancing the development and evaluation of college teaching: A commentary on Cavanagh. *Innovative Higher Education, 20*(4), 241–247.

Bernstein, D. (1998). Putting the focus on student learning. In P. Hutchings (Ed.), *The course portfolio: How faculty can examine their teaching to advance practice and improve student learning* (pp. 77–83). Sterling, VA: Stylus.

Bernstein, D. (2002). Representing the intellectual work in teaching through peer-reviewed course portfolios. In S. F. Davis & W. Buskist (Eds.), *The teaching of psychology: Essays in honor of Wilbert J. McKeachie and Charles L. Brewer.* Mahwah, NJ: Lawrence Erlbaum.

Bernstein, D., Burnett, A. N., Goodburn, A., & Savory, P. (2006). *Making teaching and learning visible: Course portfolios and the peer review of teaching.* Bolton, MA: Anker.

Bernstein, D., Jonson, J., & Smith, K. (2000). An examination of the implementation of peer review of teaching. In K. E. Ryan (Ed.), *New directions for teaching and learning: No. 83. Evaluating teaching in higher education: A vision for the future* (pp. 73–86). San Francisco, CA: Jossey-Bass.

Bess, J. L. (2000). Tasks, talents, and temperaments in teaching: The challenge of compatibility. In J. L. Bess & Associates, *Teaching alone, teaching together: Transforming the structure of teams for teaching* (pp. 1–32). San Francisco, CA: Jossey-Bass.

Bess, J. L., & Associates. (2000). *Teaching alone, teaching together: Transforming the structure of teams for teaching.* San Francisco, CA: Jossey-Bass.

Biggs, J. B. (2003). *Teaching for quality learning at university* (2nd ed.). Buckingham, UK: Society for Research into Higher Education & Open University Press.

Blackburn, R. T., & Lawrence, J. H. (1995). *Faculty at work: Motivation, expectation, satisfaction.* Baltimore, MD: Johns Hopkins University Press.

Boyer, E. L. (1990). *Scholarship reconsidered: Priorities of the professoriate.* Princeton, NJ: Carnegie Foundation for the Advancement of Teaching.

Braskamp, L. A. (2000). Toward a more holistic approach to assessing faculty as teachers. In K. E. Ryan (Ed.), *New directions for teaching and learning: No. 83. Evaluating teaching in higher education: A vision for the future* (pp. 19–33). San Francisco, CA: Jossey-Bass.

Braskamp, L. A., Brandenburg, D. C., & Ory, J. C. (1984). *Evaluating teaching effectiveness: A practical guide.* Beverly Hills, CA: Sage.

Braskamp, L. A., & Ory, J. C. (1994). *Assessing faculty work: Enhancing individual and institutional performance.* San Francisco, CA: Jossey-Bass.

Cashin, W. E. (1996). *Developing an effective faculty evaluation system* (Idea Paper No. 33). Manhattan, KS: Kansas State University, Center for Faculty Evaluation and Development.

Ceci, S. J., & Peters, D. (1982, September). Peer review: A study of reliability. *Change, 14*(6), 44–49.

Center for Educational Design and Assessment. (n.d.). *The meta-profession project.* Retrieved January 5, 2007, from www.cedanet.com/meta/#matrices

Centra, J. A. (1975, May/June). Colleagues as raters of classroom instruction. *Journal of Higher Education, 46*(3), 327–337.

Centra, J. A. (1993). *Reflective faculty evaluation: Enhancing teaching and determining faculty effectiveness.* San Francisco, CA: Jossey-Bass.

Centra, J. A. (1994, September/October). The use of the teaching portfolio and student evaluations for summative evaluation. *Journal of Higher Education, 65*(5), 555–570.

Centra, J. A. (2000). Evaluating the teaching portfolio: A role for colleagues. In K. E. Ryan (Ed.), *New directions for teaching and learning: No. 83. Evaluating teaching in higher education: A vision for the future* (pp. 87–93). San Francisco, CA: Jossey-Bass.

Chickering, A. W., & Gamson, Z. F. (1987, June). Seven principles for good practice in undergraduate education. *AAHE Bulletin, 39*(7), 3–7.

Chism, N. V. N. (2003). Using evaluation to enhance faculty performance and satisfaction. In D. R. Leaming (Ed.), *Managing people: A guide for department chairs and deans* (pp. 179–203). Bolton, MA: Anker.

Chism, N. V. N. (2004). Characteristics of effective teaching in higher education: Between definitional despair and certainty. *Journal of Excellence in College Teaching, 15*(3), 5–36.

Chism, N. V. N. (2005). Promoting a sound process for teaching awards programs: Appropriate work for faculty development centers. In S. Chadwick-Blossey & D. R. Robertson (Eds.), *To improve the academy: Vol. 23. Resources for faculty, instructional, and organizational development* (pp. 314–330). Bolton, MA: Anker.

Chism, N. V. N. (2006, July/August). Teaching awards: What do they award? *Journal of Higher Education, 77*(4), 589–617.

Cobb, K. L., Billings, D. M., Mays, R. M., & Canty-Mitchell, J. (2001, November/December). Peer review of teaching in web-based courses in nursing. *Nurse Educator, 26*(6), 274–279.

Cohen, P. A., & McKeachie, W. J. (1980). The role of colleagues in the evaluation of college teaching. *Improving College and University Teaching, 28*(4), 147–154.

Cosser, M. (1998, March). Towards the design of a system of peer review of teaching for the advancement of the individual within the university. *Higher Education, 35*(2), 143–162.

Cox, M. D., & Richlin, L. (Eds.). (2004). *New directions for teaching and learning: No. 97. Building faculty learning communities.* San Francisco, CA: Jossey-Bass.

Donald, J. G. (2000). The pedagogue: Creating designs for teaching. In J. L. Bess & Associates, *Teaching alone, teaching together: Transforming the structure of teams for teaching* (pp. 35–61). San Francisco, CA: Jossey-Bass.

Donald, J. G. (2002). *Learning to think: Disciplinary perspectives.* San Francisco, CA: Jossey-Bass.

Eisner, E. W. (2001). *The educational imagination: On the design and evaluation of school programs* (3rd ed.). Englewood Cliffs, NJ: Prentice Hall.

Elbow, P. (1980). One-to-one faculty development. In J. F. Noonan (Ed.), *New directions for teaching and learning: No. 4. Learning about teaching* (pp. 25–40). San Francisco, CA: Jossey-Bass.

Electronic portfolios for faculty evaluation. (2005, November). *Academic Leader, 21*(11), 2, 8.

Elton, L. (1996). Criteria for teaching competence and teaching excellence in higher education. In R. Aylett & K. Gregory (Eds.), *Evaluating teaching quality in higher education* (pp. 33–40). London, UK: Falmer Press.

Feldman, K. A. (1989, April). Instructional effectiveness of college teachers as judged by teachers themselves, current and former students, colleagues, administrators, and external (neutral) observers. *Research in Higher Education, 30*(2), 137–194.

French-Lazovik, G. (1981). Peer review: Documentary evidence in the evaluation of teaching. In J. Millman (Ed.), *Handbook of teacher evaluation* (pp. 73–89). Thousand Oaks, CA: Sage.

Glassick, C. E., Huber, M. T., & Maeroff, G. I. (1997). *Scholarship assessed: Evaluation of the professoriate.* San Francisco, CA: Jossey-Bass.

Gmelch, W. H. (1993). *Coping with faculty stress.* Newbury Park, CA: Sage.

Golin, S. (1990). Four arguments for peer collaboration and student interviewing: The master faculty program. *AAHE Bulletin, 3*(4), 9–10.

Gray, P., Diamond, R., & Adam, B. (1996). *A national study on the relative importance of research and undergraduate teaching at colleges and universities.* Syracuse, NY: Syracuse University, Center for Instructional Development.

Gregory, K. (1996). The evaluation of the teaching of individual academics in higher education: Progress toward a construct. In R. Aylett & K. Gregory (Eds.), *Evaluating teaching quality in higher education* (pp. 1–13). London, UK: Falmer Press.

Hammersley-Fletcher, L., & Orsmond, P. (2004). Evaluating our peers: Is peer observation a meaningful process? *Studies in Higher Education, 29*(4), 489–504.

Handal, G. (1999). Consultation using critical friends. In C. Knapper & S. Piccinin (Eds.), *New directions for teaching and learning: No. 79. Using consultants to improve teaching* (pp. 59–70). San Francisco, CA: Jossey-Bass.

Hativa, N., & Goodyear, P. (2002). Research on teacher thinking, beliefs, and knowledge in higher education: Foundations, status and prospects. In N. Hativa & P. Goodyear (Eds.), *Teacher thinking, beliefs, and knowledge in higher education* (pp. 335–359). Boston, MA: Kluwar.

Hativa, N., & Marincovich, M. (1996). *New directions for teaching and learning: No. 64. Disciplinary differences in teaching and learning: Implications for practice.* San Francisco, CA: Jossey-Bass.

Howard, J. (Ed.). (2001). *Michigan Journal of Community Service Learning: Service-learning course design workbook.* Ann Arbor, MI: University of Michigan, Center for Community Service and Learning.

Hoyt, D. P., & Pallett, W. H. (1999). *Appraising teaching effectiveness: Beyond student ratings* (Idea Paper No. 36). Manhattan, KS: Kansas State University, Center for Faculty Evaluation and Development.

Huber, M. T. (2004). *Balancing acts: The scholarship of teaching and learning in academic careers.* Sterling, VA: Stylus.

Huber, M. T., & Hutchings, P. (2005). *The advancement of learning: Building the teaching commons.* San Francisco, CA: Jossey-Bass.

Hutchings, P. (1994, November). Peer review of teaching: From idea to prototype. *AAHE Bulletin, 47*(3), 3–7.

Hutchings, P. (Ed.). (1995). *From idea to prototype: The peer review of teaching: A project workbook.* Sterling, VA: Stylus.

Hutchings, P. (1996a). *Making teaching community property: A menu for peer collaboration and peer review.* Sterling, VA: Stylus.

Hutchings, P. (1996b, June). The peer review of teaching: Progress, issues, and prospects. *Innovative Higher Education, 20*(4), 221–234.

Hutchings, P. (Ed.). (1998). *The course portfolio: How faculty can examine their teaching to advance practice and improve student learning.* Sterling, VA: Stylus.

Hutchings, P. (2000). *Opening lines: Approaches to the scholarship of teaching and learning.* Menlo Park, CA: Carnegie Foundation for the Advancement of Teaching.

Hutchings, P., & Shulman, L. S. (1999, September/October). The scholarship of teaching: New elaborations, new developments. *Change, 31*(5), 10–15.

Jafari, A., & Kaufman, C. (Eds.). (2006). *Handbook of research on eportfolios.* Hershey, PA: The Idea Group.

Johnson, T. D., & Ryan, K. E. (2000). A comprehensive approach to the evaluation of college teaching. In K. E. Ryan (Ed.), *New directions for teaching and learning: No. 83. Evaluating teaching in higher education: A vision for the future* (pp. 109–123). San Francisco, CA: Jossey-Bass.

Kane, J. S., & Lawler, E. E. (1978). Methods of peer assessment. *Psychological Bulletin, 85*(3), 555–586.

Katz, J., & Henry, M. (1988). *Turning professors into teachers: A new approach to faculty development and student learning.* Phoenix, AZ: American Council on Education/ Oryx Press.

Keig, L. (2000, March). Formative peer review of teaching: Attitudes of faculty at liberal arts colleges towards colleague assessment. *Journal of Personnel Evaluation in Education, 14*(1), 67–87.

Keig, L., & Waggoner, M. D. (1994). *Collaborative peer review: The role of faculty in improving college teaching* (ASHE-ERIC Higher Education Report No. 2). Washington, DC: The George Washington University, Graduate School of Education and Human Development.

Knapper, C., & Cranton, P. (Eds.). (2001). *New directions for teaching and learning: No. 88. Fresh approaches to the evaluation of teaching.* San Francisco, CA: Jossey-Bass.

Knapper, C., & Wright, W. A. (2001). Using portfolios to document good teaching: Premises, purposes, practices. In C. Knapper & P. Cranton (Eds.), *New directions for teaching and learning: No. 88. Fresh approaches to the evaluation of teaching* (pp. 19–29). San Francisco, CA: Jossey-Bass.

Lewis, K. G. (2001). Using an objective observation system to diagnose teaching problems. In K. G. Lewis & J. T. P. Lunde (Eds.), *Face to face: A sourcebook of individual consultation techniques for faculty/instructional developers* (pp. 115–134). Stillwater, OK: New Forums Press.

Ludwick, R., Dieckman, B. C., Herdtner, S., Dugan, M., & Roche, M. (1998, November/December). Documenting the scholarship of clinical teaching through peer review. *Nurse Educator, 23*(6), 17–20.

Malik, D. J. (1996, June). Peer review of teaching: External review of course content. *Innovative Higher Education, 20*(4), 277–286.

Massy, W. F., Wilger, A., & Colbeck, C. (1994, July/August). Overcoming "hollowed collegiality." *Change, 26*(4), 11–20.

Menges, R. J. (1991). *Why hasn't peer evaluation of college teaching caught on?* Paper presented at the annual meeting of the American Educational Research Association, Chicago, IL.

Menges, R. J., & Associates. (1999). *Faculty in new jobs: A guide to settling in, becoming established, and building institutional support.* San Francisco, CA: Jossey-Bass.

MERLOT. (2006a). *About us.* Retrieved January 14, 2007, from http://taste.merlot.org/

MERLOT. (2006b). *Evaluating criteria for peer reviews.* Retrieved January 30, 2007, from http://taste.merlot.org/evaluationcriteria.html

MERLOT. (2006c). *Peer review rating system.* Retrieved January 14, 2007, from http://taste.merlot.org/ratingsystem.html

Miller, R. I., Finley, C., & Vancko, C. S. (2000). *Evaluating, improving, and judging faculty performance in two-year colleges.* Westport, CT: Bergin & Garvey.

Millis, B. L. (1992). Conducting effective peer classroom observations. In D. H. Wulff & J. D. Nyquist (Eds.), *To improve the Academy: Vol. 11. Resources for faculty, instructional, and organizational development* (pp. 189–206). Stillwater, OK: New Forums Press.

Millis, B. L. (2006). Peer observations as a catalyst for faculty development. In P. Seldin & Associates, *Evaluating faculty performance: A practical guide to assessing teaching, research, and service* (pp. 82–95). Bolton, MA: Anker.

Moody, J. (2005, April). *Rising above cognitive errors: Guidelines for search, tenure review, and other evaluation committees.* Keynote presented at the WEPAN/NAMEPA joint conference, Las Vegas, NV.

Muchinsky, P. M. (1995). Peer review of teaching: Lessons learned from military and industrial research on peer assessment. *Journal on Excellence in College Teaching, 6*(3), 17–30.

Murray, J. P. (1995). *Successful faculty development and evaluation: The complete teaching portfolio* (ASHE-ERIC Higher Education Report No. 8). Washington, DC: The George Washington University, Graduate School of Education and Human Development.

Nordstrom, K. (1995). Multiple-purpose use of a peer review of course instruction program in a multidisciplinary university department. *Journal on Excellence in College Teaching, 6*(3), 125–144.

Nutter, D. O., Bond, J. S., Coller, B. S., D'Allesandri, R. M., Gewertz, B. L., Nora, L. M., et al. (2000, February). Measuring faculty effort and contributions in medical education. *Academic Medicine, 75*(2), 200–207.

O'Neil, C., & Wright, A. (1995). *Recording teaching accomplishment* (5th ed.). Halifax, Nova Scotia: Dalhousie University.

Paulsen, M. B. (2002). Evaluating teaching performance. In C. L. Colbeck (Ed.), *New directions for institutional research: No. 114. Evaluating faculty performance* (pp. 5–18). San Francisco, CA: Jossey-Bass.

Perlman, B., & McCann, L. I. (1996). *Recruiting good college faculty: Practical advice for a successful search.* Bolton, MA: Anker.

Pister, K., & Sisson, R. (1993). *The Pister Report: Lessons learned—The aftermath of the report of the task force on faculty roles and rewards in the University of California.* Paper presented at the first annual American Association for Higher Education Conference on Faculty Roles and Rewards, San Antonio, TX.

Pratt, D. D. (1997, July). Reconceptualizing the evaluation of teaching in higher education. *Higher Education, 34*(1), 23–44.

Pritchard, R. D., Watson, M. D., Kelly, K., & Paquin, A. R. (1998). *Helping teachers teach well: A new system for measuring and improving teaching effectiveness in higher education.* Lanham, MD: Lexington Books.

Quinlan, K. M. (1996, June). Involving peers in the evaluation and improvement of teaching: A menu of strategies. *Innovative Higher Education, 20*(4), 299–307.

Rice, R. E., Sorcinelli, M. D., & Austin, A. F. (2000). *Heeding new voices: Academic careers for a new generation* (New Pathways Working Paper No. 7). Sterling, VA: Stylus.

Richlin, L. (2006). *Blueprint for learning: Constructing college courses to facilitate, assess, and document learning.* Sterling, VA: Stylus.

Richlin, L., & Manning, B. (1995a). Evaluating college and university teaching: Principles and decisions for designing a workable system. *Journal on Excellence in College Teaching, 6*(3), 3–15.

Richlin, L., & Manning, B. (1995b). *Improving a college/university teaching evaluation system: A comprehensive developmental curriculum for faculty and administrators* (2nd ed.). Pittsburgh, PA: Alliance.

Robertson, D. R. (2003). *Making time, making change: Avoiding overload in college teaching.* Stillwater, OK: New Forums Press.

Root, L. S. (1987, March). Faculty evaluation: Reliability of peer assessments of research, teaching, and service. *Research in Higher Education, 26*(1), 71–84.

Ryan, K. E. (Ed.). (2000). *New directions for teaching and learning: No. 83. Evaluating teaching in higher education: A vision for the future.* San Francisco, CA: Jossey-Bass.

Schuster, J. H., & Finkelstein, M. J. (2006). *The American faculty: The restructuring of academic work and careers.* Baltimore, MD: Johns Hopkins University Press.

Scriven, M. (1973). The methodology of evaluation. In B. R. Worthen & J. R. Sanders (Eds.), *Educational evaluation: Theory and practice* (pp. 60–104). Belmont, CA: Wadsworth.

Seldin, P. (1984). *Changing practices in faculty evaluation.* San Francisco, CA: Jossey-Bass.

Seldin, P. (1993a, October). How colleges evaluate professors: 1983 v. 1993. *AAHE Bulletin, 46*(2), 6–8.

Seldin, P. (1993b). *Successful use of teaching portfolios.* Bolton, MA: Anker.

Seldin, P. (2004). *The teaching portfolio: A practical guide to improved performance and promotion/tenure decisions* (3rd ed.). Bolton, MA: Anker.

Seldin, P. (2006). Building a successful evaluation program. In P. Seldin & Associates, *Evaluating faculty performance: A practical guide to assessing teaching, research, and service* (pp. 1–19). Bolton, MA: Anker.

Seldin, P., & Associates. (2006). *Evaluating faculty performance: A practical guide to assessing teaching, research, and service.* Bolton, MA: Anker.

Sell, G. R., & Chism, N. (1988). *Assessing teaching effectiveness for promotion and tenure: A compendium of reference materials.* Columbus, OH: The Ohio State University, Center for Teaching Excellence.

Shore, B. M., Foster, S. F., Knapper, C. K., Nadeau, G. G., Neill, N., & Sim, V. (1986). *The teaching dossier: A guide to its preparation and use.* Montreal, Quebec: Canadian Association of University Teachers.

Shulman, L. S. (1993, November/December). Teaching as community property: Putting an end to pedagogical solitude. *Change, 25*(6), 6–7.

Shulman, L. S. (1996, November). The pedagogical colloquium: Focusing on teaching in the hiring process. *AAHE Bulletin, 49*(3), 3–4.

Shulman, L. S. (2005). *The pedagogical colloquium: Three models.* Retrieved January 4, 2007, from the University of California–Irvine's Electronic Educational Environment web site: http://eee.uci.edu/news/articles/0512colloquium.php

Smith, R. (2001). Formative evaluation and the scholarship of teaching and learning. In C. Knapper & P. Cranton (Eds.), *New directions for teaching and learning: No. 88. Fresh approaches to the evaluation of teaching* (pp. 51–62). San Francisco, CA: Jossey-Bass.

Sorcinelli, M. D. (1984). An approach to colleague evaluation of classroom instruction. *Journal of Instructional Development, 7*(4), 11–17.

Speer, A. J., & Elnicki, D. M. (1999, April). Assessing the quality of teaching. *American Journal of Medicine, 106*(4), 381–384.

Stake, R. E., & Cisneros-Cohernour, E. J. (2000). Situational evaluation of teaching on campus. In K. E. Ryan (Ed.), *New directions for teaching and learning: No. 83. Evaluating teaching in higher education: A vision for the future* (pp. 51–72). San Francisco, CA: Jossey-Bass.

Strenski, E. (1995). Two cheers for peer review: Problems of definition, interpretation, and appropriate function. *Journal on Excellence in College Teaching, 6*(3), 31–49.

Taylor, P. G., & Richardson, A. S. (2001). *Validating scholarship on university teaching: Constructing a national scheme for external peer review of ICT-based teaching and learning resources.* Canberra, Australia: Commonwealth of Australia, Department of Education, Science and Training.

Tiberius, R. G., & Tipping, J. (2000). The discussion leader: Fostering student learning in groups. In J. L. Bess & Associates, *Teaching alone, teaching together: Transforming the structure of teams for teaching* (pp. 108–130). San Francisco, CA: Jossey-Bass.

University of Nebraska–Lincoln. (n.d.). *Peer review of teaching project.* Retrieved January 4, 2007, from www.courseportfolio.org/peer/pages/index.jsp

University of Saskatchewan. (2003). *Framework for peer evaluation of teaching at the University of Saskatchewan: Best practices.* Saskatoon, Saskatchewan: Author.

Walcerz, D. B. (1999, April). *Enable OA: A software-driven outcomes assessment process consistent with the principles of good practice for assessing student learning.* Paper presented at the ASEE mid-Atlantic Conference, West Long Branch, NJ.

Wenger, E. (1999). *Communities of practice: Learning, meaning, and identity.* Cambridge, UK: Cambridge University Press.

Wenger, E., McDermott, R., & Snyder, W. M. (2002). *Cultivating communities of practice: A guide to managing knowledge.* Boston, MA: Harvard Business School Press.

Williams, B. C., Litzelman, D. K., Babbott, S. F., Lubitz, R. M., & Hofer, T. P. (2002, February). Validation of a global measure of faculty's clinical teaching performance. *Academic Medicine, 77*(2), 177–180.

Williams, R., & Tollett, J. (1998). *The non-designers web book: An easy guide to creating, designing, and posting your own web site.* Berkeley, CA: Peachpit Press.

Woodroof, J. B., & Searcy, D. L. (2004). Managing faculty data at the University of Tennessee: The SEDONA project. *EDUCAUSE Quarterly, 27*(1), 36–44.

Index